GOD'S ANSWER FOR PRESSURE

Also available from Bridge Publishing, Inc.
by Eric Hayden:

God's Answer for Fear

DEDICATION

Dedicated to my grandchildren
Miriam, Matthew and Ruth
with the prayer that "in Christ" they may never
succumb to the pressures of this world.

CONTENTS

INTRODUCTION ix

THE PRESSURE OF . . .
1. ARTIFICIALITY 1
2. AVOIDANCE 7
3. BUSYNESS 13
4. CIRCUMSTANCES 19
5. CONFORMITY 25
6. DEFEAT 31
7. DISHONESTY 37
8. DOUBT 43
9. HARDSHIP 49
10. HELPLESSNESS 55
11. HOPELESSNESS 61
12. HUMANISM 67
13. IDEALISM 73
14. IGNORANCE 79
15. INSECURITY 85
16. INCONSTANCY 91
17. INADEQUACY 97
18. INFLUENCES 103
19. INSENSITIVITY 109
20. IMMATURITY 115
21. IRRELEVANCY 121
22. MATERIALISM 127
23. MORTALITY 133
24. PROGRESS 139
25. RESTITUTION 145
26. SELF-EFFORT 151
27. TIMIDITY 157
28. TOGETHERNESS 163
29. UNCERTAINTY 169
30. WORLDLINESS 175
31. YESTERYEAR 181

INTRODUCTION

The pace of life in the twentieth century takes its toll on both Christian and non-Christian. Speed, noise, mechanization, these and much else have had disastrous effects on marriage and family relationships. Not even ministers, missionaries, and clergy have been exempt from the influences of our hectic world.

Books have appeared off the Christian press to try and combat the trend of succumbing to pressure: *How to Manage Pressure Before Pressure Manages You*, *Pressure Can Either Make or Break Us*, and so on. Such books usually are of a psychological or psychiatric nature, even though they may have a scriptural or spiritual slant. By contrast the aim of this present work is to be wholly scriptural, concentrating on the Pauline phrase "in Christ." Thirty-one occurrences of this phrase in the letters of the apostle Paul enable the reader to understand and cope with pressure on a daily and monthly basis.

GOD'S ANSWER FOR PRESSURE

Pressure *can* either make or break us. It can be good as well as bad. There is the pressure of the pile driver that results in a solid foundation for a tall building. There is the pressure of the paper clip that holds important documents together. Then there is the pressure of the housewife's iron that results in a carefully smoothed shirt. On the other hand there is the pressure of the clamp applied to a suspect's thumb or finger by unscrupulous interrogators, resulting in a false confession.

In my book *God's Answer for Fear* (Bridge Publishing, Inc., 1985) I explained how some kinds of fear are healthy, enabling us to ward off danger and disease. In the same way a certain amount of pressure enables us to live lives that are stable and strong. Pressure *can* be beneficial.

At the Carnegie Institute of Technology in Pittsburgh, scientists have in this decade generated the highest sustained pressure ever achieved under laboratory conditions—2.7 million atmospheres, or approximately 40 million pounds per square inch. The experiment was made in an effort to produce metallic hydrogen. Scientists believe that hydrogen can become a metal when subjected to intense pressure. But pressure in such a controlled environment is quite different from pressure in an explosive setting, such as the detonation of an atom bomb. In the same way, in our personal, mental, and emotional lives, pressure can exert such an influence that we are "blown apart," whereas if

INTRODUCTION

the same pressure is under the control of Christ, if we are *in Christ,* as Paul puts it, then the pressure can be beneficial and become a blessing, bringing us deeper into Christ. Then the pressures of life will make us and not break us.

Sometimes the apostle writes "Christ in us" and sometimes "we in Christ." The two expressions are interchangeable according to theologians, who frequently refer to the phrase as "Christ-mysticism." That does not mean that there is an air of mystery about the phrase or the experience; it is *reality,* not mystery! The phrase describes an intimate relationship that is both thrilling and rewarding. It is the believer's moment-by-moment, day-by-day enjoyment of the presence and power of Jesus Christ. Christ becomes dominant in all we think, say and do. It was this kind of intimate relationship that enabled Paul to withstand the pressures of persecution, privation, and imprisonment.

The German pastor Dietrich Bonhoeffer discovered the same truth. While imprisoned by the Nazis, with a daily diet of only crusts of bread thrown through the cell "Judas" window (and coffee that was one third grounds), he continued to read his *Losungen* (daily Bible readings published by the Moravians). On August 21, 1945, the day he was executed, his last remaining words about that morning's meditation are recorded: "The key to everything is in the 'in Him.' All that we may rightly expect from God, and ask Him for, is to be found in Jesus Christ."

GOD'S ANSWER FOR PRESSURE

This living "in Christ" helps us as individuals to live in a world of stress and strain, giving us help, comfort, and assurance on dark days. Life becomes Christ-centered instead of self-centered. This intimate relationship is the fulfillment of the apostle's words, "Not I, but Christ lives in me." We live in Him; He lives in us; self recedes into the background.

In 1956 I gained my Master of Arts degree from the University of Durham. My two-year research resulting in my accepted thesis was into the Pauline conception of baptism with special reference to his doctrine of Christ-mysticism. To put it more simply, it was a study of "in Christ" and believer's baptism. Naturally it was a serious academic study of the phrase "in Christ," but ever since then I have tried to live by the spiritual experience, not the scholarly academic understanding of the phrase, and have found throughout thirty-six years of Christian ministry the experience has been a daily adventure. It has been a day-by-day climb of thrilling mountain slopes, with, however, the downward paths into the valleys below when I have failed to follow my Savior closely or neglected to hear His voice saying, "Follow Me."

Jesus wants to be in me and in you, and He wants us to be in Him. The more we live in Christ, the less perplexing and dangerous pressures will become. Pressures from without and pressures within, so common to us all in these days, will be countered by

INTRODUCTION

living in Christ as He lives and reigns in us, Lord and King of our hearts and minds. First, of course, there must be a finding of Christ and an accepting of Christ before we can go on to living in Christ and fulfillment in Christ. So pray this prayer before beginning your daily adventure of living in Christ, God's answer for pressure:

O God, You have prepared for those who love You many good things that surpass our understanding. Bless me each day as I meditate on your Word. Grant that I may know in all its fullness that union of mind, heart, and soul with Jesus Christ my Savior which will give me grace and power to fulfill my duties towards my fellowmen.

Chapter One

THE PRESSURE OF ARTIFICIALITY

The promise of life which is in Christ Jesus.
2 Timothy 1:1

It sometimes is said that a young man does not know the girl he is marrying until he sees her early in the morning the day after the wedding! Previously she was always wearing make-up, and at her best. Now he sees her for the first time in the cold light of day. And she sees him as well.

Artificial eyelashes, artificial nails, artificially colored hair, cosmetic dentistry, and cosmetic surgery; the list of modern artificiality is endless.

There is nothing artificial about the Christian life however. After finding Christ there comes acceptance: "As many as received [accepted] Him, to them gave he power to become the sons [or daughters] of God" (John 1:12). To accept Him means life, real life with no artificiality.

GOD'S ANSWER FOR PRESSURE

God never forces His gifts on us. He freely offers; it is up to us to freely accept. God is sovereign and He could force us to accept, but side by side with divine sovereignty goes human responsibility.

Real life in Christ! If you have accepted Him then He's there, *in you*. His resurrection life has become the very life you live. His mind becomes your mind; His personality has become your personality; His reactions become your reactions. Think of it: the One who created life lives His own life in and through you. Complete union *with* Christ means complete control *by* Christ. And we can have this real life because God has promised it: "the promise of life which is in Christ Jesus."

Notice how Paul tells us that the *promise* is "in Christ" as well as the *life* is in Him. This promise runs right through Scripture. It was given in the Garden of Eden as soon as the first man sinned and died spiritually. It is there right through to the book of Revelation where man stands in the very vestibule of eternity.

This is the kind of life that we each desire in our heart of hearts. "Good Master," said a rich young ruler to Jesus, "what must I do to inherit eternal life?" The answer of Jesus to that question was given to another: "I am come that they might have life, and that they might have it more abundantly." "More abundantly" could be translated, "without artificiality."

On the shelves in any supermarket, product after

THE PRESSURE OF ARTIFICIALITY

product is labelled "no artificial flavoring" "no artificial colors." When we read such words we know we are buying the pure, unadulterated fruit juice or whatever else we are shopping for. How few lives are there like that. Environment, circumstance, and background can result in artificial smiles, words, actions, and even relationships. So many people wear a mask and the true face is not seen. Others are always role-playing and so we never know the real person or where we stand with them. Thus life becomes unreal, with some playing one part and others another.

Now there is natural, physical life, and there is supernatural, spiritual life. Which is the real kind of life? Well, physical life ends with death; spiritual life continues throughout all eternity. Both kinds of life begin with a birth, either our physical birth, through our mother, or the "new birth," a process engendered by the Holy Spirit. Physical life is characterized by walking and talking, eating and drinking, sleeping and waking, and working and playing. In the spiritual life these have their counterparts: walking along the highway of holiness; talking in prayer and preaching; eating and drinking through Bible study and fellowship; sleeping and waking in backsliding and revival; working in Christian service. How very real the spiritual life is when shed of its artificiality.

Ordinary physical life is a wonderful thing. "It feels good to be alive" we say when in perfect health and it is a sunny day. But the spiritual life is even more wonderful, for it is life in Christ. Augustine said, "Join thyself to the eternal God, and thou wilt be eternal." Physical life is for earth and time alone; spiritual life is for earth and heaven, time and eternity. As God breathed into Adam and he became a living soul, so the Holy Spirit in-breathes anyone accepting Christ on the basis of repentance and faith and so restores the Creator-creature relationship.

It is wrong to compartmentalize our lives. That is truly artificial. Bible reading, prayer, hymn-singing, church attendance—these should never be put in one compartment with eating, sleeping, working, visiting friends put into another compartment. Christ knew no such artificial division and those who are in Christ must live as He lived. Everything we do in life should be as sacred as our baptism or our observance of the Lord's Supper, for we do "all to the glory of God." Our daily work should be as much a preistly ministration as our Sunday School teaching. The whole of life is sacramental when we accept Christ and live in Him and He lives in us. Genie Price could even make a slimming diet sacramental! She took the view that to pass over attractive, fattening foods was a love-offering to the Lord!

One of the simple pleasures my wife and I indulge in on a free day is to visit a nearby tourist town and re-discover a little-known beauty spot. It is called "The Prospect." It is a sheltered garden on a cliff top

THE PRESSURE OF ARTIFICIALITY

and overlooks one of England's most beautiful rivers, the Wye. The river twists and turns for many miles and then at Ross-on-Wye almost turns back on itself in a great horse-shoe wind. Do you know why a river takes such a winding path? It twists and turns as it descends from the mountain source to the sea, taking the least line of resistance.

If we stand on "the mount of God," daily living above the artificiality of the world below, we shall see it for what it is. We shall understand that the Christian life is a "race to be run and a fight to be fought" and not taking the line of least resistance.

Looking beyond the horse-shoe bend of the river Wye, my wife and I can see the Welsh and Herefordshire hills in the distance. As the Psalmist we "lift up our eyes to the hills" and see that our help comes from the Lord who made them. There is nothing weak and crooked about the hills and mountains as there is with the meandering river below. The river bends to the hills. We must not give into the pressure of artificiality. We must be "strong in the Lord and in the power of His might."

Such a life is hard, but being a life in Christ, it is worth it. As a small boy in Sunday School I was taught to sing H.W. Longfellow's hymn:

> Tell me not in mournful numbers,
> 'Life is but an empty dream.'
> Life is real, life is earnest.

It is real if we resist the pressures of artificiality.

GOD'S ANSWER FOR PRESSURE

Dear God, Creator and Life-giver, I thank You for Jesus Christ, whom to know is life eternal. Help me to live so that every thought, word and deed will be an act of true worship. Make my life holy and helpful to my fellowmen, a genuine godly life in an artificial world.

Chapter Two

THE PRESSURE OF AVOIDANCE

In the sight of God speak we in Christ.
2 Corinthians 2:17

Michael was an up-and-coming executive, and an out-and-out Christian. He was 35 years of age and had been in Christ since the age of twenty.

On one of his frequent business trips overseas he sat next to a much older, more prosperous looking executive. As they were served their meal, they began a conversation, and Michael soon brought it around to spiritual things. In a few simple sentences he explained God's plan of salvation. The older man's reaction was, "If there are as many Christians in the world as I have been led to believe, then why hasn't someone told me this sooner!"

"Silence is golden" states the adage. "Silence is sinful" would be more scriptural, for we read in the Bible: "Let the redeemed of the Lord say so!"

Yes, life and lip go together if we are in Christ. Living in Christ means taking every opportunity of speaking about Christ. Our close relatives and friends have perhaps never heard us speak about our wonderful Savior and His wonderful love. Why not? Have we not been under the pressure of avoidance?

How easy it is to avoid witnessing for our Savior and Friend. Avoidance tactics do not have to be learned at some spiritual military academy—they are inbuilt into us. We avoid the opportunities of witnessing to the unsaved by withdrawing from the world, by keeping company with only those of "the household of faith." When opportunities do present themselves we think of such awful excuses as, "It's wrong to thrust religion down other people's throats," or "I can witness by my life. What I do, my acts and actions are more eloquent than my lips speaking." True, sometimes a good life does impress the non-Christian. It portrays only the *fruit* of the Christian faith, however, and not the *root*. A good life does not set forth and explain the doctrines of repentance, conviction, faith, conversion, and regeneration. Only the tongue can do that, backed up, of course, by a life that tallies.

"I can leave all that to the preacher, he's been trained to do it." Wrong! That is another avoidance tactic. "All witnesses" is the keynote of the New Testament Christians. The preacher must study and be taught in public speaking, rhetoric, elocution, and homilitics, but the ordinary Christian who has

THE PRESSURE OF AVOIDANCE

not been called into the full-time ministry must be a witness, as faithfully as the preacher is a herald.

Acts 8:4 states, "They went everywhere preaching." The word for "preaching" in this verse means literally "gossipping," something that most people do all too frequently, without having to take lessons in it. And remember, when Paul said "in the sight of God speak we in Christ" he was not writing a preacher's letter to another preacher (as he does when writing to Timothy or Titus). He was writing to ordinary Christians, many of them slaves, living in Corinth.

God is omniscient, all knowing and all seeing, and Paul reminds the Corinthians of this. He sees when we are silent and He sees when we are speaking, so being in Christ we *must* speak.

Of course it is difficult. Most of us are shy, retiring, or reserved. But we can make those traits of character another avoidance tactic. So if you are crying out, "Who is sufficient for these things?" remember the secret is to be so identified with the Savior, so influenced and controlled by Him at all times, that He will create the right opportunities and then give the very words to say. Much harm can be done by *making* opportunities instead of *taking* them. And much harm comes through speaking in our own strength instead of in His, that is speaking in Christ.

To know when to remain silent is as important as knowing when to speak. Job's comforters were at

GOD'S ANSWER FOR PRESSURE

their best when they remained silent for seven days and nights! Some people we come into contact with need few words at first but rather a sympathetic smile, a firm grip on the arm, a handshake, or even an arm around the shoulder. Once physical contact has been made, reassurance given, and love expressed, then will come the right time to speak.

When the opportunity to speak is taken then we must speak in Christ, that is, in His power, under His control, knowing His mind, as He guides. Nervousness, reserve, being shy, all these and more do not matter if we are in Christ, for Jesus said, "Take no thought how or what ye shall speak: for it shall be given you in that same hour what ye shall speak. For it is not ye that speak, but the Spirit of your Father who speaketh in you" (Matthew 10:19, 20). Like Paul we shall be able to speak "with boldness, as [we] ought to speak."

Speaking boldly does not mean offensive outspokenness. Speaking in Christ we shall speak with courtesy, with humility, with meakness, trying at all times not to give offense. Our aim must never be to win an argument, for we might win the argument and lose our friend. Winsomely we should want to win over our friend. We must be courteous and considerate, listening to our friend's point of view before putting our own. In fact, as an ambassador of Christ, we should not be presenting our own views, but sharing God's Good News. We must shun debate and argument that might give offense or

THE PRESSURE OF AVOIDANCE

antagonize our friend. We must at all times speak in the spirit of love.

A man once went to hear the famous preacher Dr. Guthrie of Scotland. Never having seen the preacher he asked when a man entered the pulpit, "Is that Guthrie who has come into the pulpit?" His neighbor replied, "I dinna ken and dinna care: I came here to worship God!" So as we learn to witness for Christ, in Christ, we shall decrease and He will increase. He will be heard and seen and not ourselves. It will be a case of "hearing a voice but seeing no man." We shall be hidden behind the cross, the center and core of our gospel message.

So do not preach *at* your friends and workmates. Speak *to* them and *with* them, just as Jesus spoke to people when He was on earth.

Take a real interest in people's work, their hobbies, their pleasures, their problems, their children, their private lives, and their workaday lives. These will become the stepping stones along which you will walk into fuller friendship so that you can speak "of God in Christ." Sharing their interests will create a bridge between you, over which you will both cross and meet in the middle on common ground.

Jesus was known as a friend of tax-gatherers and sinners. He must be our motivating force as well as our example. He alone can give the wisdom and the words. The more we live "in Him" the more we shall have to witness about and the less silent

GOD'S ANSWER FOR PRESSURE

we shall remain. So don't give in to the pressure of avoidance. Instead, let Jesus give you His power and strength, making up every deficiency of nature so that your Christ-controlled words will result in others resisting the pressure of avoidance of Christ and receiving Him gladly as Savior and Lord.

Lord, speak to me, that I may speak
In living echoes of Thy tone;
As thou hast sought, so let me seek
Thy erring children, lost and lone.

O teach me, Lord, that I may teach
The precious things Thou dost impart;
And wing my words, that they may reach
The hidden depths of many a heart.
      Frances Ridley Havergal

Chapter Three

THE PRESSURE OF BUSYNESS

> For we are his workmanship, created
> in Christ Jesus unto good works.
> Ephesians 2:10

Jesus Christ made us, for "without Him was not anything made that was made." When we accepted Him then He made us all over again. Some call the experience conversion, making a decision, commitment, or being born-again. Perhaps regeneration is the best term of all for it means literally re-generation, or to generate again. The Oxford English Dictionary defines it as "to come into renewed existence," or "spiritually re-born." Scripture puts it: "If any man is in Christ he is a new creation," or "we are His workmanship."

How wonderful it is to be made into new men and women! "Behold, I make all things new." By accepting Christ we have new desires, new habits, new friends, and acquire a new set of values. But notice how Paul emphasizes that this change for the better is for "good works." Although we have not been saved by works but by God's grace, through faith, we are saved for good works after our re-creation. Faith is the *root* of Christianity but works are the *fruit*.

A small boy was given a watch by his father. Being very young it was not a real watch. It was in an attractive case and the hands moved round when turned with the winding knob. It had no spring or battery and so did not move by itself.

At night the little chap put it under his pillow, the hands pointing to six o'clock. In the morning he looked at it and saw that it was still six o'clock. At church the next Sunday he seemed to be paying more attention than usual to the preacher's sermon. When asked why over Sunday lunch he said, "The preacher was talking about my watch." "What do you mean son?" asked father. "Well," said the boy, "he spoke about face without works is dead!"

How close to the truth. Yes, *faith* without works is dead, like a watch with no works. That is the theme of the letter of James in the New Testament. Real, genuine faith in Christ results in good works. If not, then our faith is a sham.

So very often we are too busy to perform these good works. Paul reminds us that we should do "good to those of the household of faith" and then "to all men." But the pressure of family commitments,

THE PRESSURE OF BUSYNESS

those at home and relatives near at hand and further away, often leaves little time for benevolent and philanthropic works to others. And sometimes when we do find time to do them then we get in a hurry and flurry over them. Bustling about with busyness is not the way to serve the Prince of Peace. If we are to do our good works in Christ then we are to do them unobtrusively not ostentatiously, with humility, gentleness, patience, and tranquility.

It has been said that in Scripture we read that "Jesus went about doing good," and we often just go about! We hurry and bustle here and there and get next to nothing done. We have no routine for good works as we have for household chores. Our benevolence is often a spasmodic effort rather than a continuous one. No wonder good works have been described as "an inescapable characteristic of the regenerate life." It is doing all the good we can, in every way we can, to everybody we can. We must not let the pressure of worldly busyness distract us from Christ's work.

How often we are wrapped up in overhauling the car, cleaning the house, scurrying to the mall, or sitting at home glued to the television. All the time there are widows and orphans (James's special group in need of our good works) and other needy people who should have our undivided attention. There are prisons and hospitals to be visited; children's homes and orphanages; dinners to provide for the hungry and lonely;

GOD'S ANSWER FOR PRESSURE

and many aged people who need visiting.

No wonder Paul uses the word "workmanship." Literally it means "a work of art" or a "masterpiece." So the person "in Christ" is meant to be viewed by others as they would view a work of art in a gallery.

In one of the churches I pastored, a local beauty queen was converted. She certainly was a "masterpiece" as far as looks, beauty, and deportment went. Walking past the church one day she had heard us broadcasting over our public address system testimonies, songs, readings from Scripture, and a short gospel talk. All her popularity and success as a beauty queen had not satisfied her deepest need, and she was drawn to the church where she found Christ, accepting Him as Savior and Lord.

Her conversion hit the headlines of the local newspaper. Visited by a reporter, she showed him the Bible she now kept in her case of beauty aids, and told how she was studying God's Word at home and in church. And her favorite chorus became, "Let the Beauty of Jesus be Seen in Me."

Gradually, the beauty contests faded out of her life. The parade of boyfriends and admirers gave way to only one and resulted in marriage. Years later I visited the church and learned that she was bringing her first child up in a Christian home and also was teaching the Bible to others. She had become a "masterpiece of good works" as she formerly had been a masterpiece of earthly works.

THE PRESSURE OF BUSYNESS

Not all of us could enter beauty contests for our looks are anything but handsome. We can take heart when we look at some of the people God has used in the past. Thickset Moody, stubborn-chinned Spurgeon, and one-eyed Christmas Evans, so mightily used to revive the eighteenth century chapels of Wales. We can, however, be a masterpiece of good works, taking the time out from the busyness imposed by the world and become willing to "spend and be spent" for Christ.

It means discipline is needed in all spheres of the Christian life. For some it will mean a shake-up of lifestyle; for others it may mean taking a sheet of paper and writing down a list of good works that come to mind and then setting right priorities. It may mean writing up our diaries differently so that certain days or evenings are set aside for helping others.

We are to be masterpieces, and each one an original. None of us are to be reproductions. We possess individuality, and the rare gift of expressing our uniqueness. Remember, God is "the Great Original" and it is He Who has accepted us in Christ.

Holy Spirit, help me today in my walk and work. May I do those good works that will help others and bring glory to your name. Help me to do them quickly and quietly, patiently, and with a tranquil heart and mind. Help me to increase in obedience and usefulness, a masterpiece of your grace.

Chapter Four

THE PRESSURE OF CIRCUMSTANCES

Rejoice in Christ.
Philippians 3:3

When we find Christ, we also find real joy. By becoming a Christian, a man or woman in Christ, we do not subscribe to a long list of "thou shalt nots"; rather our newfound faith results in getting, not giving up; receiving, not rendering up, this and that. Even if there is something you think you have to relinquish, then be sure you will receive much more in its place.

C.S. Lewis described his Christian conversion as *Surprised by Joy*—"religion never was designed to make our pleasures less!"

It is this inestimable joy of life in Christ that the apostle points out to believers in Philippians, a letter referred to as *Joy Way* by a well-known Bible commentator (Guy King, Keswick Convention speaker). Paul urges Christians to "rejoice, and again I say, rejoice." Yet Paul was writing from prison, a place where pressure is surely felt more than in many other places.

Richard Wurmbrand spent fourteen years in communist prisons and endured much torture. In his book *Tortured for Christ* he has a chapter with the title "How we could be joyful—even in prison!" He describes how non-Christian prisoners and his communist guards often were astounded at the way Christians could be happy while undergoing much privation and terrible suffering. He states, "We could not be prevented from singing, although we were beaten for this" and likened himself to a nightingale that would sing even though it knew that at the end of the song it would be killed. In other words, he could not help but be joyful.

Where the man of the world looks for happiness in outward things such as pleasure, amusement, sport, theatre, or television, the man in Christ can be full of joy without such artificial aids. How? The Christian's joy comes from within. It is not dependent upon outward circumstances. The man in Christ has an inner source of joy like a bubbling spring, deep within his innermost being.

For many years a popular British radio program has been Desert Island Discs. Well-known personalities are invited to the studio to say how they would cope with boredom if stranded for an indefinite period on a desert island. They are allowed only a

THE PRESSURE OF CIRCUMSTANCES

few books and a few discs or records. The stipulation about the books is that the Bible cannot be included in their choice.

A friend of mine, a Christian, Chairman of the International Miners' Mission, Dr. Shewell-Cooper, was invited to take part in the program. He was a well-known horticulturalist and one-time head gardener to the Queen, but little did he say about gardening books on the program. Since he could not choose the Bible he chose *Matthew Henry's Commentary on the Bible!* Little did the radio interviewer realize that in the seven volumes of *Matthew Henry* the very words of Scripture, the whole Bible, were included, as well as the comments, verse by verse, by Matthew Henry.

Dr. Shewell-Cooper pointed out that even on a desert island, where the pressure of circumstances was great (loneliness, solitude, strange and frugal food, adverse weather conditions, etc.) it was possible to be joyful. Even without *Matthew Henry's Commentary* I know Dr. Shewell-Cooper would have been full of joy, for he had "hid God's Word in his heart" since he firmly believed in memorizing Scripture verses and passages.

Whatever our pressure of circumstances, sickness, sorrow, solitude, set-backs, the "slings and arrows of outrageous fortune" (Shakespeare)—in Christ we still can be joyful. Joyful rather than happy, for happiness depends on what happens, as the Sunday School chorus points out—

GOD'S ANSWER FOR PRESSURE

I'm happy when ev'rything happens to please,
But happiness comes and goes.

But, by contrast—

While the heart that is stayed on Jesus
  the Savior
Ever with joy o'erflows;
Happiness happens, but joy abides,
In the heart that is stayed on Jesus.

H.H. Lemmel

The non-Christian pays to get happiness. The Christian's joy is free. It comes as a result of being in Christ. It is part of our spiritual inheritance when we were adopted into the family of God.

Worldly happiness is transient, it does not last. Soon after the play is over or the holiday has ended, we are back into the real world again and the pressure of circumstances. The smile is wiped off the face and gloom settles upon our thoughts. Drugs, drink, magazines, novels, records, films, plays—none of these can give a lasting transformation. But Christ can!

When we find Christ we not only find *a* Savior but we find He is *the* Savior and *such* a Savior. Daily we receive life in all its fullness from Him so that even "mourning is turned into joy."

A pastor friend of mind went to visit an elderly lady who lived alone in a remote country cottage. As he approached the front door he saw that it was open. Drawing near he heard talking and stopped

THE PRESSURE OF CIRCUMSTANCES

outside in case she had a visitor. He soon realized that she was saying grace before having her midday meal. "Thank You, Father, for all this and Jesus too," she prayed. The "all this" was a crust of dry bread (no butter) and a small piece of cheese! In spite of old age, arthritis, deafness, difficulty in seeing, loneliness, and much more—the pressure of outward circumstances—she was full of joy, a joy from deep within because she belonged to Jesus; she was "in Christ" and so could "rejoice in Christ."

Might it not also have been that she was thanking God for His marvellous world of nature. Her front door was open, and her outlook was across green fields to the hills beyond. Like the hymn writer, G.W. Robinson, we soon find after finding Christ that "heaven above is softer blue" and "earth around is sweeter green." Our eyes see beyond the difficult circumstances around us in home, office, factory, school, college, as we see Jesus in all His beauty. Such joy puts a spring into our step and causes summertime in the heart when it is wintertime in the world. Such joy makes us want to burst into song, singing—

> *Jesus, Thou joy of loving hearts,*
> *Thou fount of life, Thou light of men;*
> *From the best bliss that earth imparts,*
> *We turn unfilled to Thee again.*
>
> Latin hymn, 12th Century
> Translated by Ray Palmer

GOD'S ANSWER FOR PRESSURE

I thank You, Jesus, that I can say with one of old, "Happy is he who has the God of Jacob for his help." In the midst of dark and depressing circumstances I can look up and see that God is in his heaven and all's right with the world. Help me also to look within and see my Savior, the altogether lovely one. So may I sing for joy, bringing joy and happiness into the lives of others.

Chapter Five

THE PRESSURE OF CONFORMITY

My ways which be in Christ.
                 1 Corinthians 4:17

Accepting Christ means more than accepting Him as Savior. It means accepting Him as Lord and thus accepting to live His way. He says to us, "This is the way, you walk in it." The early Christians were known as followers of the Way. So must we be.

A legitimate translation of Paul's words "my ways which be in Christ" would be, "the path I tread in Christ Jesus," or "my method of proceeding in Christ." What Paul is doing in this letter is something that you and I dare not do. He is sending Timothy to the Corinthians to remind them of the kind of life he, Paul, lives in Christ. They are being told to copy or imitate his life in the Lord. Would that we lived on such a high level in Christ that others could be asked to imitate us. In those days people could copy

Paul's walk and work, his words and deeds, his character and conduct. His whole manner of life, as a Christian, as a pastor and teacher, and as an evangelist and missionary, was such that others could safely copy him. Paul wrote to them and sent Timothy to them that they might conform to his pattern.

Young people are always being asked to conform. In one decade they may be expected to conform to a certain kind of dress and behavior and in another decade that same dress and standards of behavior appear "old hat" and out of date.

In came long, shoulder-length hair and Carnaby Street clothes, real or reproduction military uniforms. Then came flaired trousers, the brightly-dyed hair style of the punk rockers. While young people try to give the impression they are rebelling and "doing their own thing," going against conforming to pattern, they are in fact conforming, but to a different standard. Instead of conforming to their parents' ideal image for them they are conforming to their own ideas for themselves. They rebel against school uniform (liked by their parents for its "snob value") but they dress alike and look alike in other clothes: jeans, sweaters, leather jackets, and so forth.

Whatever the standard set, whatever the model or pattern followed, the pressure of conformity is heavy indeed for young people coping with other pressures of adolescence.

THE PRESSURE OF CONFORMITY

When I served in the British army during the Second World War I talked with many Christians who hated their army service. It was not so much they were adopting pacifist principles, it was conformity that hit them hard. Many had been university undergraduates, used to living a life of independence. Their manner of life, dress, and friendships was their own affair. They had left behind home, parental guidance, and discipline.

Having tasted freedom and independence, now in the army, they were being asked to conform again. They hated the sameness of the uniform, being given a number and rank. There was no way in which personalities could be expressed through clothing. "The army does your thinking for you," they were told. All they had to do was to obey orders, sometimes given by officers with less academic and intellectual attainments than their own. All this was far more soul-destroying than primitive living conditions or even bloodshed on the battlefield.

Now in peace time there is the pressure to conform. People are divided into types: the old-school-tie type, the brigade-of-guards type, the foreign-office-type, the civil service or local government type. But the Bible urges us not to be "conformed to this world"—not conformed but transformed! How is that possible? By conforming in a different way, by conforming to Christ's pattern for us. The early Christians were

GOD'S ANSWER FOR PRESSURE

so called "Christ-ones" first in Antioch. The people of Antioch suddenly saw disciples of Jesus Christ so resembling Him that they nicknamed them Christians. Could the inhabitants of our hometown give us the same nickname? Instead of being pressed into a materialistic mold by the world, are we transformed men and women, living our lives as people-in-Christ-types?

Paul was writing to Christians who had found Christ and accepted Him by faith, but they were not conforming to His ways. They were, for instance, split into factions. Christ's way is the way of unity and harmony, not discord and division.

The secret to relieving the pressure of worldly conformity is to conform to Christ's image. As we live in Him we receive the encouragement and enabling power, to copy Christ and imitate Him in all things.

Nathaniel Hawthorne has an interesting story. A boy called Ernest was told by his mother that there was a legend concerning the valley in which they lived. "Someday," she said, "there will arise a man, born in this neighborhood, whose countenance will resemble the Great Stone Face which looks out from the side of that distant mountain." Ernest looked out at the craggy rocks that portrayed naturally the features of a fine and noble man. Every day of his life he looked in the village for a human face that resembled the face in the rock. Always he was disappointed.

THE PRESSURE OF CONFORMITY

As he grew up Ernest became a fine person, earning the love and respect of the community. One evening, near the end of his life, as he was speaking to a group of neighbors, his face was lit up by the setting sun. "Look," said one of them, "Ernest resembles the Great Stone Face!" It was true. While looking for the resemblance in another, Ernest himself had come to conform to the face in the cliff.

In the same way, as we allow Christ to take over our lives and accept Him fully, we shall overcome the pressure of conforming to the world's ideas and ideals and become conformed to His image, walking in His ways.

Walking implies progression and constancy. It is progressively and constantly putting one foot a step in front of the other. Stop that simple pattern and you stop, motionless. So when we stop walking in Christ's ways we become motionless in the Christian life. And where there is no progress there is no prosperity in the spiritual life.

"Do your converts stand?" an evangelist was asked. "I hope not," he replied, "for they should be following on to know the Lord!"

The secret of walking, of living in the ways of Christ is to dwell deeper in Him daily. Through prayer, get to know His mind and will about everything you do. Then do it (or say it) as you know He would do it or say it. He's a Person, not a set of principles to live by; a Person who has been found, accepted, and now imitated as closely as possible.

GOD'S ANSWER FOR PRESSURE

Dear Lord, may nothing mar my ways in Christ. Help me in all my ways to acknowledge You, walking humbly with you. Help me to think Your thoughts, walk in Your ways, and so live my life by Your standards that I shall be conformed to Your eternal righteousness.

Chapter Six

THE PRESSURE OF DEFEAT

>Now thanks be unto God, which always causeth us to triumph in Christ.
>
>2 Corinthians 2:14

Do you frequently know defeat in your daily life? The Christian is not promised a bed of roses. Life is a battleground, not a sports field, for the one in Christ. Ranged against us are the pressures of the world, the flesh and the devil. Often we seem to come off worst.

We need not be like the Grand Old Duke of York's men—"When they were up, they were up, and when they were down, they were down." We need not be up in the spiritual heights one moment and down in the depths (or dumps) another. Life need not be a see-saw existence, conquering a bad habit one minute and being conquered by it the next. We are meant to be "more than conquerors."

GOD'S ANSWER FOR PRESSURE

By accepting Christ as Savior and living in Him we have the means of mastery. Through accepting His victory on the cross, victory is available for us.

The Duke of Wellington once declared that the greatest tragedy in the world was a defeat. But Rudyard Kipling said: "I have known defeat, and mocked it as we ran." That is more in keeping with the teachings of the apostle Paul. He could thank God that in Christ he always triumphed.

Your life and mine is meant to be like a Roman triumph in which the returning general led his victorious army in procession. Chained to his chariot were the captives, the prisoners of war. Accompanied by the wafting of incense the procession wended its way beneath the victory arch. It was the highest military honor in Roman times. So the person who is in Christ can live in a state of victory over the pressure of defeat, marching triumphantly through life, overcoming faults and failings, sins and shortcomings. This was the hallmark of genuine Christian living for Paul. Wherever we are, whatever we are doing, God can cause us to triumph in Christ.

In over thirty-six years of pastoral ministry I have often had to counsel teenagers (other age-groups as well, but teenagers especially) with the problem of the pressure of defeat. Sometimes I ask them to fill in a questionnaire with these questions included:

THE PRESSURE OF DEFEAT

1. Did you feel rejected by one of your parents (this to a teenager who has left home)?
2. Did you feel pressured by parents to attain the same standards as an elder brother or sister (I experienced this myself: I was expected to be the same kind of athlete and tennis player as my elder brother, but I was never as good as him)?
3. Did you have long periods of illness that kept you away from school, so that your grades suffered?
4. Were you sent away from home to a boarding school where you could not cope?
5. Did teachers embarrass you in front of the class?
6. Did your parents move often (to other parts of the country) so you had to keep making new friends?
7. Did your parents expect you to act, speak, and generally conduct yourself in an adult way before you were ready for it?
8. Were you bullied at school?
9. Was your privacy not respected at home?
10. Was your first experience of the opposite sex embarrassing?

Most teenagers respond affirmatively to these questions. The result is the pressure of defeat, the failure to come up to expectations, the disappointment they feel themselves and believe they have caused their parents.

GOD'S ANSWER FOR PRESSURE

Only an understanding of what it realy means to be in Christ (even in teenage years) can change defeat into victory. The way to experience such "triumph in Christ" is to follow the late Dr. Donald Barnhouse's pattern of dividing the day into seven sections, looking ahead only one section at a time, asking God to keep and sustain you until the next section. When the devil has been active during a service I am conducting I have to do this for myself. I divide the service into quarter-hours, for I find I can battle against Satan in the power of the Spirit for that period of time better than for an entire hour or more at a time. Once God has given the victory for the first quarter then it is easier for the next, and so on.

So trust God to give you the victory from breakfast time to when you begin school, college, or work. Then until mid-morning. Then until lunch. Then until afternoon break. Then until time to go home. Then while relaxing or doing homework until supper. Then the late evening until bedtime. You must work out the seven sections that are most convenient for you.

Before you begin the next section always look back and thank God for the victory over defeat He has given you in the section just completed. It's like going for a walk in the country. Look only from tree to tree, bend in the road to the next bend, and so on, enjoying God's natural world in which He has placed you. In this way you will become "committed to a life of victory," as one preacher used to put it.

THE PRESSURE OF DEFEAT

Believe in victory in the midst of defeat, believing enough to claim it and make it actual. "This is the victory, even your faith," says God's Word. Take a concordance and look up every reference to victory in the spiritual life that you can find and mark them in your Bible, then memorize them.

Of course, victory only comes after a battle, victory being the outcome of warfare that both sides strive for. It may come after you have been running, for the athlete who breaks the tape first is acknowledged as victor. It may come only through running *away*. Learn to recognize the voice of the Spirit who will tell you when to resist and when to run.

We are surrounded on every side by evil principalities and powers. They will do their utmost to defeat us, causing us to lose our joy and leave us in a spirit of spiritual depression. The Psalmist knew such depression, as did the prophet Jonah and Jeremiah and others. When you have such a "black mood," and Satan seems nearer than your Savior, remember how Christ defeated Satan once and for all on the cross. Now that you have accepted Him you can share in that triumph. Remember, you are, as a Christian soldier, clothed in impregnable armor, front and back, head to toe, with "the whole armor of God."

An old Puritan saint sums it up well: "Be occupied with Him." Get to know Christ; talk to Him, love Him, serve Him, live in Him and enjoy Him. It is not be occupied with *it*, that is defeat and depression. It is not becoming preoccupied with a method or an experience. It is being occupied with a Person, knowing that He is in you and you in Him.

O Lord God, overshadow me with Your love amidst all the difficulties, doubt, and darkness of this life. Reveal to me more and more the privileges of continuous fellowship with my Savior, which will enable me to triumph over the world, the flesh, and the devil.

Chapter Seven

THE PRESSURE OF DISHONESTY

I say the truth in Christ.

Romans 9:1

Would you take the oath in a court of law? The Friends or Quakers would not. Perhaps no one in Christ ought to do so, for Christ told us not to swear by anything but to let "our yes be yes, and our no be no." No Christian should contemplate misleading a judge or jury. Nor should we be guilty of telling "white" lies. Surely all lies are black!

Many people who do take the oath on the witness stand commit perjury, which is punishable by law. They plead innocent and are then found guilty, the long list of untruths being revealed.

Maybe we do not do anything wrong that takes us into a court of law. Well, what about false entries on our annual income tax forms? Or what about the unfounded malicious gossip we so delight in passing

GOD'S ANSWER FOR PRESSURE

on, having already told the one who told us, "My lips are sealed, of course I won't pass it on?"

Advertisers take advantage of human gullibility by sometimes making false and outrageous claims for their products. And even preachers and evangelists tend to exaggerate attendance counts "evangelistically speaking."

What a wonderful thing it would be if everyone spoke the truth all the time. The pressure of dishonesty always is with us. As small children we tell lies to escape punishment. As grown men and women we tell lies to advance ourselves, perhaps to gain a better position in the firm for which we work. Not every line of a resumé is to be believed by the panel about to interview a list of candidates. Many of us tend to overestimate our talents in a job even if we do not end our application with, "I'm just the person you want!"

Fiona started attending my evening gospel services with a bunch of young college students. Not a student herself, and not having the potential for the academic life, she started hanging round with them "talking big." We found her out in several lies.

Soon she was off to London as she was sure she could make good there. We suggested she attend a certain well-known church where we knew the late Dr. Graham Scroggie (an author and Bible expositor) was to hold a series of services. After her first Sunday in London she wrote me a letter saying she had been to the church, had heard Dr. Scroggie,

THE PRESSURE OF DISHONESTY

and had "gone to the front" in answer to his appeal (or altar call), and we would be happy to know that she was now a Christian.

Just as I was about to write Fiona a letter, saying how glad I was, and then to go on and encourage her in the Christian life, I had a phone call. It was a minister friend of mine who had had a free Sunday and so went to hear Dr. Scroggie. I told him about Fiona and he quickly said, "But Dr. Scroggie did not give an invitation to enquirers to come to the front!"

Fiona, it appeared, was a pathological liar, a condition that necessitated psychiatric treatment. Happily she did become genuinely coverted to Christ and overcame her tendency to lie.

The apostle Paul, when writing to Rome to the band of Christians there, described his disappointments and admitted his despondency because of the reluctance of his countrymen to respond to the gospel. Because he was in Christ he "spoke the truth in Christ." He would not have found acceptance in many of our present day ministers' fraternals where when one is asked, "How is the work going?" and the reply always seems to be, "Oh, quite encouraging, thank you!" We should really tell the truth as Paul did and confess that we are not seeing conversions, we are in need of a heaven-sent, Holy Spirit revival, but such is the human heart, even the regenerate human heart, we tend to exaggerate. Such exaggeration is equivalent to untruthfulness.

GOD'S ANSWER FOR PRESSURE

The pressure of being looked on as unsuccessful, however, has caused us to be dishonest.

Being in Christ we are living in the One who declared Himself to be "the way, the truth, and the life." How then can we be untruthful when the truth lives in us and we live in Him? Would He make untruthful excuses about the work He was doing? Was it not said of one period of His earthly ministry "He could do no mighty work there?" His was not a ministry of "converts at any price and I'll prolong the meeting until I get some."

Even the world has a proverb that says, "Honesty is the best policy," although more people quote it than live by it. That is why banks have to have their pens chained to the desks. Without that chain the pens would soon become "mislaid." No! not mislaid—stolen! I know of a so-called Christian father (only a nominal Christian, I am afraid) who used to encourage his children "to beat the system." If they could get away with half-fare on the buses and trains when they had grown above the age limit for such concessions, then he encouraged them to do so.

"What is truth?" begins Lord Bacon's essay, quoting the words of the Roman governor, Pilate, who tried Jesus before sentencing Him to be crucified. Pilate was not answered in words, for Truth was personified before Him—Jesus *was* truth. How dare we, His followers, speak anything less than the truth, instead falling prey to the pressures of dishonesty. As it used to be said

THE PRESSURE OF DISHONESTY

"a gentleman's word is his bond" so the word of a Christian must be utterly reliable.

Since Christ is the Searcher and the Reader of hearts, He knows when we speak falsely, and He is deeply grieved. No wonder Paul's words have been accepted by some Bible commentators as equivalent to such a phrase as "Cross my heart and hope to die." When Paul said "I say the truth in Christ" he was speaking with hand on heart and every word was true.

Millions long to be beautiful and spend a great deal of time and money on beauty aids. Do millions long to be truthful?

Thousands long to be successful and go to night school after working hours to better themselves. Do thousands long to be truthful?

Hundreds long to be peaceful and join peace organizations with the object of bringing in an era of peace into our troubled and violent world. Do hundreds long to be truthful?

Many Christians long to be fruitful, successful servants of God extending His kingdom and enlarging His church. Do they long to be truthful?

It is "the truth that makes us free." The living Word, Jesus who is the Truth, and the written Word (the Bible—"truth unchanged, unchanging") that can make us free from the pressure of dishonesty. As we say "Amen," the word of ratification, at the end of our prayers, so we ought to be able to say "Amen" to every word and sentence that we speak,

GOD'S ANSWER FOR PRESSURE

for we must as those who live in Christ "speak the truth in Christ."

O God of truth, implant Your truth in our hearts and minds. Make us daily more conformed to Christ who is the Truth. Forgive us for all past lies and deception.

Chapter Eight

THE PRESSURE OF DOUBT

> The covenant, that was confirmed before of God in Christ.
> Galatians 3:17

Are you a Doubting Thomas? Do you ever have doubts that you have found Christ, or that He has ever called you, or that you are living in Him? John Bunyan's Doubting Castle is a frequent place of residence for many Christians.

Sometimes we feel that the need most pressuring us is the need for ratification of our faith in Christ. "Ratification" or "establishment" is what Paul's word means, translated "confirmed" in the King James Version. God the Father does this work of ratification by confirming His covenant. God entered into a solemn covenant (agreement or transaction) with Abraham. Four hundred years later He gave the law to Moses, but this law did

GOD'S ANSWER FOR PRESSURE

not contradict the original covenant, but rather established or confirmed it.

The divine promise to Abraham was that he and his descendants would be blessed by God and that from Abraham's descendants would come the Messiah. Abraham accepted this promise by faith, believing that God kept His promises. By a "new covenant," drawn up at Calvary, God again promised blessing to generations of mankind. This new covenant, confirmed at Calvary, includes you and me and all who have found the secret of living in Christ. As Abraham had many descendants so Christ has many spiritual children, sons and daughters adopted into His family as a result of their faith in Him.

But we must keep our side of the agreement. This we do by living up to His laws. We are saved by faith, not by commandment keeping. But as saved men and women we willingly keep the commandments, and the very fact that we want to do so and do indeed do so is part of our confirmation that we are in Christ. We refrain from blasphemy and adultery, we keep God's day holy, we honor our parents, we do not submit to covetousness and greed and all the other doubtful pressures of the materialistic world in which we live, because we have found Christ and are living in Him. His presence in our lives is the restraining influence that our modern world of law-breakers know nothing about, and seemingly do not want to know about. But we who

THE PRESSURE OF DOUBT

are in Christ delight in doing His will, abiding by His laws. This is our witness to the reality of our faith, serving also to confirm us in that faith, even when the pressure of doubt dismays us.

Simon lived under a constant weighty pressure of doubt. He had gone out from my church as a missionary to Brazil. The missionary society found him very unsatisfactory and put him on a ship for home. He jumped ship and also tried to jump off a bridge. He was next put on a plane and watched until it was safely on its way to England.

He could not understand the attitude of the mission board. The pressure of doubt became greater when they suggested that a psychiatrist see him. He refused. The board wrote to me to ask me to give hospitality to a Christian psychiatrist and to invite Simon to meet him as a friend and not in a professional capacity. I felt I had to agree to this and the meeting took place. His diagnosis was that Simon was schizophrenic.

By now he was leaving his parents' home around midnight, going for walks in the country. He would carry a hand-bell and ring it as he walked the lanes. He then believed he could walk on water. He began hearing voices. He refused to take the medicine his doctor prescribed for him on the advice of the psychiatrist.

Voices in his head told him to fast and he would get better. Rapidly he began to lose weight. His parents locked the front and back doors at night

GOD'S ANSWER FOR PRESSURE

and slept with the keys beneath the pillows. He found a way out through a window on several occasions.

One evening I visited him with one of my elders. On the way there we stopped at a fried fish and chip shop. Putting his portion on Simon's knees, my elder said, "Simon, in the name of Jesus Christ break your fast and eat." Like a small boy Simon ate up all the fish and every single chip! Soon he was eating normally again.

As the missionary society still was somewhat wary of him, Simon decided to return to Brazil and go out as a missionary on faith lines, trusting in God for his support. He soon married, had children, and remained in his adopted country serving the Lord for fifteen or more years.

What pressures from doubt resulted from his illness. There were not only his own personal doubts ("Why is God allowing this to happen to me?") there were the doubts in the minds of the church members who were supporting him in prayer, who had seen him grow up as a boy, become converted, enter the university, serve the Lord, and then offering himself as a missionary in Brazil. And, there was the severe pressure exerted by doubt in the minds of his parents.

All were in Christ, the patient, the parents, the praying fellowship of the church. And there is no other solution for the alleviation of grave doubts. When the aggressive agnostic or atheist at our place

THE PRESSURE OF DOUBT

of work asks "Why does God allow tragedies to happen?", such doubts can only be understood when we are in Christ.

The stained glass window in a church building can look dusty, muddy, uninteresting, or even covered over with a protective netting when viewed from the outside. On entering the building, however, the colors and design are seen in all their beauty. The benefits of the Christian life are only really discernable when we are in Christ. The onlooker cannot tell if the orange we are eating is sweet or sour. Only if he eats a piece of the orange himself will he discover if it is sweet. "O taste and see that the Lord is good."

When we have off days, when Satan delights in bombarding our minds with doubts; when we have dry spells when Satan makes it seem as if the heavens are a dome of brass and our prayers cannot penetrate it; then it is that we need to remember that for all who are in Christ God has confirmed or established the covenant or agreement between us, the covenant drawn up at Calvary. The pressure of doubt is relieved by the efficacious blood of Jesus.

What Paul is saying, in effect, is that as we found Jesus by looking to the cross in faith, that same cross is the ratification of our faith. So, on a day when the washing machine breaks down, or the traffic jams are the worst we have ever known, or a business deal fails to go through, and doubts pour into our minds and faith begins to waver—then we

GOD'S ANSWER FOR PRESSURE

take a fresh look at the cross and the dying form of our Savior. The look results in new life, life in Christ, and we take fresh heart and renewed hope and go on living and abiding in Christ.

I asked, "Are you a Doubting Thomas?" How were the doubts of Thomas dispelled? He looked at the wounds of the risen Christ. The pressure of doubt was lifted when he saw the credentials of Christ. The bloody nail prints in hands and feet were sufficient to convince him.

Heavenly Father, please give me the grace to keep Your commandments, that all may be well with me and that You may rejoice over me. Help me to overcome those habits that hinder others seeing You in me, thus doubting the reality of the life You have promised to all who believe. Grant that by Your grace I may be able to help in solving some of the problems which cause such bewilderment to many at this present time.

Chapter Nine

THE PRESSURE OF HARDSHIP

My bonds [chains] in Christ.
Philippians 1:13

When Christ first finds us we become captivated by His love. If we progress in Christ, as we should, then we desire to be His slave, becoming as Paul puts it, "a prisoner of the Lord."

Paul never considered himself to be a prisoner of the powers that be but a "bond slave" of Jesus Christ. He never dwelt on the pressures of life as an itinerant preacher and missionary. Certainly he had to endure many hardships: hunger, harsh treatment, primitive methods of travel, and undeserved imprisonment. But these circumstances he turned to good account, seizing every opportunity for personal witnessing and the preaching of the gospel.

Think of it: Caesar's court evangelized, servants and soldiers challenged with the claims of Christ.

GOD'S ANSWER FOR PRESSURE

The soldiers were probably unwilling listeners, yet a captive audience since they had their prisoner Paul chained to their wrist! No wonder Paul said that his "bonds . . . are manifest in all the palace and in all other places." Word spread from mouth to mouth. He is visited in prison by those hungry to hear about Christ and His salvation. He becomes known as a notable prisoner and a man who can show others how to find eternal life. Soldiers who would not normally enter a synagogue, and who grumbled and groused at every church parade, found that they were listening to a mighty preacher of the gospel in the line of duty. After a spell of guard duty, two on and four off (two hours guarding Paul and four free hours to catch up with cleaning equipment and catching up on sleep) what a lot they had to tell to others when they gathered in the mess hall for meals.

What opportunities we have of reaching those who never enter a church, especially those who think they are hard pressed and always bemoaning their lot. Some are tied to the kitchen sink; others find the tedium of monotonous manual work a hardship; yet more complain of commuting to work and how the time of the journey added to their working day leaves little time for leisure or pleasure. How about making the kitchen an evangelizing center? Why not invite in neighbors and friends (even the gas or electricity or telephone engineers working nearby the street) for coffee, giving them

THE PRESSURE OF HARDSHIP

some Christian literature before they leave. Why not use the traveling time to work, on bus or train (or if giving a lift to a friend in the car) as a missionary expedition, a God-given opportunity to speak a word about Jesus to a captive audience like Paul's in prison.

If you are not seizing these opportunities perhaps it is because you have found Christ as Savior but not as Lord of your life. You are in Christ, but not deeply immersed in Him as His bond-slave. Christ must be our slave-owner. "My bonds in Christ" implies that having found Him we discover that He must own us body, mind, and soul. But remember, the chains that bind us to Him are cords of love. Nothing else holds us to Him, only His love for us and the love of our hearts for Him. His is a love that cannot be broken, but of what quality is ours? Living in Christ surely implies loving Christ with fervent intensity and fierce constancy. Paul's bonds were a love that was stronger than any chain forged by a Roman blacksmith. No wonder that he describes himself as a bond slave who bears in his body the brand marks of the master, signifying complete subjection to Him. "I bear in my body the marks of the Lord Jesus" (Galatians 6:17).

Love for Jesus burned within Paul's heart as fiercely as the slave owner's hot branding-iron burned into the flesh of his slave. Thus we ought to be able to sing with J.G. Small—

GOD'S ANSWER FOR PRESSURE

I've found a Friend; oh, such a Friend!
He loved me ere I knew Him;
He drew me with the cords of love,
And thus He bound me to Him;
And round my heart still closely twine
Those ties which nought can sever,
For I am His, and He is mine,
For ever and for ever.

Are we, like Paul, "a prisoner of the Lord"? If so, then like him, we will not become bitter when the pressure of hardship looms large in our lives and circumstances seem adverse, dark or depressing. On the contrary, we will be able to rejoice in tribulation and not become resentful of it or full of self-pity. Every time Paul looked at his chains they reminded him not of his prison cell and the limitations of life but of his calling by Christ and his life in Christ. So the pressure of sickness, sorrow, solitude, separations, and much more, will send us quickly to the side of our Friend and Savior Jesus Christ.

Many great saints and heroes of the cross have discovered that the pressure of hardships has been offset by their "bonds in Christ." As Paul and his companion Silas sang spiritual songs at midnight when in prison, so Corrie ten Boom and her frail sister Betsie testified in song to their cruel Nazi guards. Ravensbruck, the notorious women's extermination camp was the scene of their incredible

THE PRESSURE OF HARDSHIP

witness to the power of the Lord giving victory over hardship.

Sitting on the lice infested straw they thought they were there for the night. Suddenly they were moved out from beneath the canvas covering to a place wide open to the sky. Beneath them was hard cinder ground. As they laid their blankets on the hard ground, watched by the S.S. guards, Betsie's sweet soprano voice lifted in song, "The night is dark and I am far from home; Lead Thou me on."

Later on in the same camp Corrie was able to organize meetings. Catholics recited the Magnificat in Latin. Lutherans whispered one of their hymns. Eastern Orthodox women chanted under their breath. Then as the crowd grew bigger and bigger Corrie or Betsie would read the Bible. Soon two such "services" were being held, one before and one after the nightly roll call. Because they were in Christ and they were the "bond slaves" of Christ, their external circumstances and hardships became secondary to their love for the Lord and the spreading of His Word.

"When the outlook is dark, try the upward look," said an old Puritan preacher. Yes, a man or woman in Christ is never "Quite well, thank you, under the circumstances" when asked how he is. A Christian is never *never* under the circumstances, he is enabled to rise above his circumstances through union with Christ. The pressure of circumstances serves merely to turn our gaze towards Christ, the

GOD'S ANSWER FOR PRESSURE

Author and Finisher of our faith, and whose bond slave we are.

Is the pressure of circumstances getting you down at this very moment? Is your prevailing hardship loneliness through loss of a loved one? Is it unemployment or early retirement and you feel on the scrap heap? Do not look down, look up; do not look within; but look to Him; do not look around at others, only look to Christ. "The best Christians I have known," said a well-known psychologist, "are the Christians who have been led through fiery trials of the world, and wear a smiling face." There can come blessings even out of buffetings, and happiness out of hardship. Nothing happens which He does not know about and which He alone permits. He knows, He loves, He cares.

While others may love the things of this world, help me, O Lord, to sever my connections and become fast bound to you as your bond slave. May all the circumstances of my daily life drive me into closer union and fellowship with You, my Savior, the one who for the joy set before him endured the cross, despising the shame.

Chapter Ten

THE PRESSURE OF HELPLESSNESS

My helpers in Christ Jesus.
Romans 16:3

Living in Christ does not impose restrictions on our enjoyment of the good things of life. "Religion never was designed to make our pleasures less." Pleasures that are legitimate, that do not harm our bodies, the "temples of the Holy Spirit," or cause weaker "brethren to stumble," can all be indulged in. Good music, art, studying nature, and so on, are all good for the Christian.

Have you ever listened to Elgar's *Enigma Variations?* The composer dedicated the work "to my friends pictured within." The music is a collection of musical portraits. In the same way, in Romans 16, the apostle Paul gives us a series of portraits-in-miniature of his personal friends. They all are "helpers in Christ," some

GOD'S ANSWER FOR PRESSURE

of them named and others unknown, but all helpers.

Isn't it a wretched feeling, that of feeling helpless. There have been two such times of helplessness that stand out in my life. The first was when my nineteen-year-old son became ill with a rare disease while a university student. After nine days of unconsciousness he came out of it but with a three-year memory gap. I felt utterly helpless. True, I could help him to regain bodily strength, but I could do nothing to restore memory.

Twelve years later he was diagnosed as having a rare form of cancer. Although I had spent over thirty-six years as a Baptist minister, during which time many of my pastoral visits were to cancer wards, now I had to watch my own son go through the trauma of chemotherapy—and I could do nothing about it.

In a more general sense we feel the pressure of helplessness as we look at world events on our television screens. Wars, violent riots, hijacking at sea and in the air, carnage on the roads, famine in the Third World with its accompanying disease and death, especially among little children. How helpless we all feel.

How helpless some of the older generation feel in the face of modern technology. The mysteries of the microchip and the computer seem beyond them. Their small grandchildren revel in it all, while they cannot catch up with it.

This same feeling of helplessness can come upon

THE PRESSURE OF HELPLESSNESS

Christians when they look at the world around them and realize the multitudes who are without Christ. They look at Billy Graham and other successful evangelists who draw men and women to Christ and then ask themselves, "But what am I doing?" or "But what can I do?" Paul gives us the answer.

The apostle points out that some Christians are called to be pastors and teachers and others evangelists or missionaries. Some are called to be deacons or elders, but *all* are expected to become "helps," ready to help others in giving support, relieving pressure, alleviating fear, and furthering the work of the gospel.

Often being a "help" is a simple, practical way of serving Christ. I began my Christian service as a boy by putting up the hymn numbers on the hymn board for the Sunday services. Who would ever have thought that it would have led to a call to the ministry in later life? Some are "helps" by giving out or collecting up the hymn books. Some can be "helps" by giving hospitality to visiting preachers or missionaries. Others can be one of the Psalmist's "doorkeepers" in the house of the Lord—perhaps a greeter welcoming the worshipers, or a janitor keeping God's house clean and tidy.

Notice that being a "help" is not just being a "helper." A "help" for Paul is an office in its own right, not just helping or assisting someone else. It is just as important putting out the chairs for the Bible study meeting as it is to be the song leader at the

GOD'S ANSWER FOR PRESSURE

meeting. You are not just helping the minister of music or the Bible teacher, you are doing your own God-given task to His glory in your own right. So whatever you do "do it as unto the Lord" and "do it with all your might."

While writing this chapter I received two newsletters. One came from a friend in Italy who has spent a lifetime there as a missionary. At seventy-seven years of age he is still "spending and being spent," although his constant companion and helpmeet, his wife, has been called home by the Lord. The other is from a man of similar age who has just relinquished his job of chief usher in the church. Throughout he directed the ushers and greeters who give out the hymnbooks, welcome the worshipers, and take up the offering, at the Sunday service. Is the missionary more important than the chief usher? Surely both have been "helps" in their own particular way.

Do even these so-called unimportant jobs in the church daunt you when mentioned, and make you feel helpless? After my boyhood experience of putting up the hymn-numbers (I used to arrive half-an-hour early before the service to do it) I was promoted and asked to become organ-blower! It was in the days before electric blowers, let alone electric organs. I had to watch a lead weight dropping, telling me the bellows were becoming empty of air. Then I had to pump like mad to get the lead weight to rise again. It never occurred to me that

THE PRESSURE OF HELPLESSNESS

I was helping the organist. But I was a "help" in my own right, and mine was one of the most important jobs in the church!

Don't let the pressure of helplessness daunt you. Remember Paul's words: "I can do all things through Christ who strengthens me." Jesus said to His disciples, "Without Me you can do *nothing*," so with Him we can do anything.

Remember our Lord's teaching about the vine and branches. He is the trunk of the vine; we are the branches (some of us only tiny twigs at the far extent of the branches). The same sap that is in the trunk also is in the branches and twigs. Not the tiniest twig is independent of the trunk. The same life principle flows through the whole vine. So when we feel weak we remember that He is strong. When we feel helpless we remember that He is the Help of the helpless. When we feel cowardly we remember He gives courage. When we become disappointed we remember that "He is not a disappointment."

Sometimes the vine has to be pruned. The process is painful but it is necessary. When sin comes in and mars our service then we have to be pruned. Even the lowliest "help" can become proud and puffed up with what we are doing, and so the pruning process has to result in our becoming humble once again.

So our Savior is not saying "Go and do *everything*" but "Go and do *something*," even though that something may seem very small in our own

GOD'S ANSWER FOR PRESSURE

eyes. Paul says that there are "diversities of gifts" and they are divided to "every man according to his several ability." Our responsibility is to be open to the Spirit, prepared to do anything He calls us to do, believing that He who calls will equip. And remember, if we do not become "helpers in Christ Jesus" we might well become hindrances!

Dear Father, make me a help in Your church, helping others to know You and love You. Fill me with a power that is not my own, that being filled with all the fullness of God, I may be able to forward Your divine purposes for mankind, extending Your kingdom and enlarging Your church.

Chapter Eleven

THE PRESSURE OF HOPELESSNESS

> If in this life only we have hope in Christ, we are of all men most miserable.
> 1 Corinthians 15:19

A well-known picture hung in my boyhood home. It was entitled *Hope*. It depicted a young blind woman playing a lyre. Every string of the instrument was broken except one. This last string the player plucked with hope.

As a young boy the message of the picture evaded me, even though my father explained it to me again and again. As a young man called up into the army during World War II, I began to understand the picture. Its meaning became clearer as a young married man and as my son, first at nineteen years of age and then in the early thirties, became seriously ill and lay at death's door. At times, during nine days of coma, and, a decade later, months of suffering from cancer, the pressures of hopelessness seemed too much to bear.

If life has treated you badly; if people, even close friends, have let you down; if the bottom seems to be dropping out of your world; if everything seems hopeless; if the poet seems to be wrong when he wrote, "Hope springs eternal in the human breast" —when all hope has gone—then remember that in Christ you can have hope in Christ. And this Christian hope is not only for this life, but for the next.

Paul, when writing to the Corinthians, was speaking of the great Christian hope of the resurrection, that after physical death we shall live again, first as disembodied spirits and then when Christ returns as those spirits joined to glorified bodies.

Hope for the man of the world is nothing more than vague expectation or desire. The Christian's hope is certainty and makes the worldlings' hope as scarcely recognizable as hope. Worldly hope is like a kite. It changes direction and height according to the wind and air currents. Christian hope depends on an unchanging Christ, He who is "the same yesterday, today, and for ever." Such hope is "sure and steadfast," for it is grounded "firm and deep" like an anchor in the sea bed.

The man in Christ (and, of course, the woman in Christ) has a hope that penetrates into the invisible and eternal world as the ship's anchor drops into the

THE PRESSURE OF HOPELESSNESS

depths of the sea. You cannot say, like the non-Christian, "My hopes were dashed to the ground," for your hope is in the eternal Christ, the unfailing Son of God, who lives in you, and you in Him, day after day.

It is this hope that enabled the apostle to go on preaching, witnessing, teaching, traveling, evangelizing, and suffering, knowing that come what may he was eternally safe and secure in Christ, that nothing could separate him from his Savior. The same hope is ours for all trials and tribulation, all suffering and sorrow. "Neither death, nor life . . . nor things present, nor things to come . . . shall be able to separate us from the love of God, which is in Christ Jesus" (see Romans 8:38, 39). Neither poverty, privation, nor peril can pressure us into a state of hopelessness while we have hope in Christ.

We can meet all life's eventualities with strength, purpose, peace of mind, and even joy, because our hope is hope in Christ. This anticipation of future resurrection and glory gives us power to live victoriously now, in Christ.

Do your friends tell you that such hope is "pie in the sky," or that you have your "head in the clouds," or that you are being "other worldly?" Then show them how your hope in Christ affects your daily living. Show them how it helps with pressing duties and passing difficulties. Let them see that this hope is one of the most practical things about your Christian faith.

GOD'S ANSWER FOR PRESSURE

Lack of hope results in misery. Lots of Christian hope results in happiness. What is the explanation? Simply this: In a sense we have already obtained what we hoped for. While awaiting our bodily resurrection, we already live with Christ's resurrection life within us. While awaiting the future joys and peace of heaven, we already have heavenly joy and peace "spread abroad in our hearts by the Holy Spirit." The world advises: "Don't count your chickens before they are hatched." The Christian knows that he can look forward with hope because he already is enjoying that for which he hopes.

The Bible urges "abound in," and the word means, "let hope lead to greater hope." Let hope bring happiness and happiness inspire more hope still. Because it is hope in Christ, it is divine hope, a gift of God, and there is no shortage with Him.

We can be like the writer of Lamentations who could say, "Therefore have I hope." We can be like the hymn-writer Jan Struther who wrote, "Lord of all hopefulness, Lord of all joy."

Jan Struther wrote twelve hymns for *Songs of Praise*, published in 1932, before the author was thirty. Although World War II would break out seven years later, and the storm clouds were even then gathering, this young woman had hope for the future. Her hope came through in the hymn quoted above and it quickly became a favorite among university students who used it frequently in their religious meetings. Jan Struther also was the author

THE PRESSURE OF HOPELESSNESS

of the novel *Mrs. Miniver*, written in the year war broke out. The film based on the book was seen again and again by young men and women who went to see it during the "black out" (when all lights had to be shrouded to prevent enemy aircraft seeing where they were over Britain) and the blitz (air-raids on London and Britain's ports, etc.). The novel and film, like hymns, inspired hope for the future, that the war would end, that the world would become a place of freedom once again.

If we lose contact with the "Lord of all hopefulness" then our hope will diminish and die and the pressure of hopelessness will weigh upon us once again. As hope dies so will happiness. But moment-by-moment, day-by-day intimate fellowship with Christ will result in a hope in Christ that brings more and more hope, and more and more happiness.

A story is told of a small girl being shown the house in Springfield, Illinois, where Abraham Lincoln once lived. The girl's mother painted a word picture of the President's greatness and how the whole nation mourned when he died. Noticing a light in one of the windows of the house the little girl said, "Look, Mommy, when Mr. Lincoln went away he left the light on!" In the same way Jesus left the light on—the light of hope. If the gospels had ended at the cross of Calvary the story would have ended in darkness. We should be like the two disciples on the road to Emmaus who were sad and downcast as they walked. But the gospels do not end at the cross. The empty tomb became the "light left on," the light of hope for us as individuals and as a world. That is the light Paul is writing about when he speaks of "hope in Christ"—faith in the crucified Christ for pardon and peace, and faith in the risen Christ for our hope of heaven and eternity. T.O. Chisholm sums it up best in "Great is Thy faithfulness"—

Pardon for sin and a peace that endureth,
Thine own dear presence to cheer and to guide;
Strength for today and bright hope for tomorrow,
Blessings all mine, with ten thousand beside!

My Father, may every hour of the day be filled with hopeful thoughts of heaven that will lighten my burdens and help me to discharge my duties and stand firm amidst all my trials. So may I enter the peace and rest of Your eternal home, having walked with You and worked for You since I first put my trust in You.

Chapter Twelve

THE PRESSURE OF HUMANISM

In Christ shall all be made alive.
1 Corinthians 15:22

E.R. Dodds was brought up in Ireland among the northern Presbyterians. Apart from learning the Lord's Prayer and saying a nighttime prayer in bed he had little religious upbringing. By the age of seventeen he had encountered religious doubt through reading a book by Robert Ingersoll. The result was that he drew up his own "creed" of "I do *not* believe in. . . ." These statements included a denial of the inspiration of the Bible and the spiritual world.

Dodds became a brilliant student at Oxford gaining a first class degree. Some years later he returned to fill the post of Regius Professor of Greek. When he married his wife her parents knew him to be an atheist and a humanist. In old age he wrote in his autobiography that at the end he regretted that "the religious dimension" had been "totally missing" in the record of his life. He had lived believing that it was possible "more or less consciously, more or less consistently," to conduct his own life. At seventeen this was "liberation"; at eighty-three he saw it as "impoverishment." Thus he lived according to the dictates of his "daemon," an obscure being who at various times and states in his life assumed command and told his body what to do.

How tragic that such a fine, intellectual mind became closed to the truths of God's Word. And this is so of so many intellectuals who call themselves humanists.

Humanism is a philosophical point of view that emphasizes human values and rational thought. It is in direct opposition to Christian beliefs and denies the Christian view of the afterlife. Humanism has a great anti-supernatural bias. It is a system of philosophy that is openly taught in schools and universities. Whereas Christian teachers and lecturers are often criticized, and penalized, for mentioning Christian values in a subject being taught other than religious knowledge, humanists are able to put across their tenets even in a math class! Thus many young people today are subject to the pressures of humanism in schools and colleges, in class and in leisure time. Class textbooks often have the same humanistic teachings

THE PRESSURE OF HUMANISM

incorporated in their pages, whatever the subject may be.

What is the solution to this pressure imposed by those who deny the afterlife and all things supernatural? For Paul it is being "alive in Christ"—"In Christ shall all be made alive." Previously he has been speaking about being alive in Christ now, that is, living in Christ day-by-day. We have seen how many pressures that eases. But now he is speaking about being made alive in Christ in the future, that is, our bodily resurrection after dying in Christ, the subject of our previous chapter. The figure of speech he uses is an agricultural one. Paul says in 1 Corinthians 15:42, "It [the human body in the grave] is sown in corruption [in a perishable state]; it is raised to incorruption [an imperishable state]: It is sown in dishonor [humiliation], it is raised in glory; it is sown in weakness, it is raised in power."

More than a hundred years ago a humanist infidel died in Hanover. Before his death he ordered that over his grave should be placed large slabs of granite, bound together with stout iron bands. On top was placed a large block of stone weighing two tons. This was inscribed on the stone: "This grave is purchased for eternity; it shall never be opened."

A small plant took root between the granite slabs. The life principle began to work. The iron bands were broken and the stones moved wider and wider apart. The plant became a mighty tree and soon the infidel's grave was open for all to see in. If so small

GOD'S ANSWER FOR PRESSURE

a seed could open a grave, how much more easily can an omnipotent God raise you and me on the day of resurrection! As God raised His own Son after Calvary so He will raise us in Christ and we shall all be made alive.

The humanists of this world may stipulate that no cross or any other Christian symbol be placed on their grave, but they cannot prevent the effects of that cross. "It is appointed to man once to die, but afterwards the judgment." A general resurrection and a universal judgment awaits all. For the one in Christ this resurrection will mean eternal life and a bypassing of the judgment seat because all our sins have been pardoned. For the humanist and atheist it will mean being sentenced to the "second death."

What a privilege awaits the man in Christ. At harvest time in the Old Testament the Jew offered his first fruits as a token of the whole. He gave them in gratitude for a good harvest. So when Christ was raised from the dead He was God's "first fruit." When we are raised at the second coming of Christ we are the remainder of these first fruits. Until that glorious day Christ's resurrection remains as the evidence that all who are in Christ will be raised to life eternal.

As a Christian, having found and accepted Christ, you are a pilgrim, walking in His ways. Resurrection, being made alive in Christ, will be the climax of your "royal route to heaven." Consider that jet airliner on the runway. Does not the law of gravity forbid that

THE PRESSURE OF HUMANISM

such a gigantic machine should rise from the ground and fly through the air? But when the engines are started up the plane slowly begins take-off. It gathers speed and soon is airborne. There still is the law of gravity to contend with, but another law has taken over—the law of aerodynamics. The resurrection of Jesus from the dead has brought into being a new spiritual law for those who are in Christ—a divine law which says that a person who is born again shall, after death, live again.

There are false religions which speak vaguely about "another life." Perhaps a person will come back to life in another form, they say, as an animal or insect. Only the Christian religion affirms, and dares to state categorically, that Christians will live forever. There is no parallel in other religions to being in Christ. This is the Christian's privilege alone. No wonder the New Testament gives more place to the doctrine of the resurrection than to any other doctrine. And no wonder that this was the message that shook the foundations of the ancient world, when the early Christians went everywhere with the Good News that "Christ is alive" and "Because He lives we shall live also." Human philosophy had never given man such a hope, and neither does it today. It was a message of beauty and power, comfort and hope for the future. By contrast humanism can offer only a brighter today, through the inventions of science: more leisure, more labor-saving devices, and so on. Thank God that in this twentieth century, living beneath the shadow of the bomb, wars, and rumors of wars, drought and disease, famine and the failure of summit talks, we have this glorious truth summed up in the creed so many repeat in their churches on Sundays: "I believe in . . . the resurrection of the body" because "I believe in Jesus Christ . . . who . . . the third day rose from the dead."

Ever-living Father, we praise You for the empty tomb and the risen Christ. Help us to live and die so that we may have a part in the resurrection of the just, that through the grave, the gateway to life, we may pass into the presence of the ever-living and reigning Lord Jesus Christ.

Chapter Thirteen

THE PRESSURE OF IDEALISM

> To them that are sanctified in Christ Jesus, called to be saints.
> 1 Corinthians 1:2

I was brought up in a home where my mother either smoothed or fluffed up the cushions as soon as a person had gotten up from chair or sofa. The old-fashioned antimacassars (protective covering or headrest for the back of a chair) were also smoothed each time so they were creaseless for the next person to recline against!

Some years after I left home I went through a very difficult period of stress. My doctor said that I was too perfectionist and meticulous. He put it down to my upbringing as a youth. I tell this not to disparage my mother, fine Christian woman that she was, rather, it shows up the habits of that time, for if I visited any of my friends' homes the pattern was

GOD'S ANSWER FOR PRESSURE

exactly the same in middle class England. Women were houseproud to a fault. Whether this was the cause of my stressful state I do not know, but I at once changed my ways and so suffered less when in stressful situations in the future.

Some parents, of course, do have too high ideals for their children. They pressure them into becoming bookworms whereas they would rather be playing outside with other children. Others are made to practice the piano, violin, or some other musical instrument when they would rather be wielding a paintbrush or baseball bat. Later in life they become mediocre players in second-rate orchestras and vow they will never force their own children to take up anything they really do not want to do. They try to fulfill, not their own ideals but the ideals their parents had for them. Frequently these ideals were unfulfilled ideals in the lives of their parents.

Today we live in a very competitive world. Top positions are much sought after. University places are much sought after. Many countries have their "brain drain" and clever intellectuals emigrate to another country where they think they will be able to fulfill their ideals without hindrance.

According to the *Oxford English Dictionary* an "ideal" is the presentation of things in a perfect form. Thus people who spend their time aiming too high are in danger of becoming obsessive. This does not mean that we must not be ambitious, but we must not become possessed by Shakespeare's

THE PRESSURE OF IDEALISM

"vaultin' ambition." By trying to reach the top at the expense of our own leisure time, or at the expense of other's feelings, we are only heading for a downfall.

What is the answer to the pressure of idealism? It is living as a sanctified (that is a "set apart") saint of Christ. But is that not idealism too? Is not a "saint" one who has reached the top in a spiritual sense?

Sanctification does not mean a holier-than-thou attitude. Sainthood is not becoming a statue in a church wall niche or a figure in a stained-glass window. The best saints are those at the factory bench, the kitchen sink, or behind the office desk, and the bus driver's wheel. Every typing-pool needs saints—people who cannot just type so many words a minute and take down shorthand, but people who recommend Christ to others by the way their live free from pressure, stress, fear, and tension.

The paradox is this: by setting our spiritual sights high and endeavoring to reach the divine high ideal of sanctification ("Be holy even as I am holy") we counteract the worldly pressure of materialistic idealism.

The process of sanctification cannot be described or understood with our finite minds. To Paul it was a mystery. As the small boy fails to understand how a brown cow, eating green grass, produces white milk. And as the growing youngster cannot grasp how brown toast and scrambled eggs for breakfast turn into living body tissue within a few hours of

GOD'S ANSWER FOR PRESSURE

being eaten, yet they enjoy milkshakes and playing football. So the young Christian, living in Christ, gradually becomes sanctified through the activity of God the Holy Spirit.

We help along the process, declares Paul, by reckoning ourselves "dead to sin." As we "reckon" so we gradually *realize* that Christ is being "made (to us) wisdom, and righteousness, and *sanctification*, and redemption." The result is not being stand-offish, disassociating ourselves from others, but like our Savior, able to eat and drink with "tax-gatherers and sinners" while keeping our own lives clean.

For some there is a spiritual crisis. It may be at a "Keswick" Convention or a conference for the deepening of the spiritual life. It may take place in church through the laying-on of hands. Or it may happen in our own bedrooms. The place does not matter so long as we experience the deepening work of the sanctifying Spirit of God so that we pass, like Paul did, "from one degree of glory to another."

Our spiritual idealism takes the sinless Savior as our example, but that does not mean that we strive to the point of exhaustion for "sinless perfection," becoming full of guilt and morbid introspection in the process. What we do is to study the saints in God's Word for our encouragement. We read about the lives of the great spiritual giants in Christian literature. We regard the lives of spiritual

THE PRESSURE OF IDEALISM

Christians who have had an effect on our lives in the past. Then, we fix our gaze our Jesus and rely on our life in Him to make us what He would have us.

How shall we know that the process of sanctification is going on in our lives? By the kind of life we live. Others will notice a change in our lifestyle. We shall speak differently. We shall do things differently. Others will come to us to seek out our help. They will want to share their pressures with us because they see us living without being under pressure.

So the more we study God's idealism for His children, the less we shall be under the pressure of the world's idealism. The more we withdraw from the doubtful pressures of the world, the more we shall be able to meet the divine idealism for the Christian. The Christian who longs to lose the pressure of idealism: getting, getting on, and getting up in the world, can do so if he truly lives "in Christ" and longs to bel sanctified in Christ daily.

It is said that Oliver Cromwell ordered the silver saints to be taken from the churches and "put into circulation." That is where the saints ought to be. They are not meant to be in safe, obscure places, but in the world of everyday life, circulating among the ungodly and showing them the privileges of the Godly.

GOD'S ANSWER FOR PRESSURE

Father, sanctify me, washing me clean from the stains of my past wrongdoing. Give me grace to put away all hurtful and harmful things, and fill me with your clean spirit, that I may bring forth the fruits worthy of repentance.

Chapter Fourteen

THE PRESSURE OF IGNORANCE

You are wise in Christ.
                        1 Corinthians 4:10

During the recent two to three decades there has occurred what is known as "a knowledge explosion." Much publicity has been given to education, the need for it and the benefits of it. Diplomas and degrees are eagerly sought after, with young people pressured into believing that no worthwhile job or profession can be entered without them. The result has been a string of letters after people's names, but often no job obtainable due to economic recession. Some people, it is said, have nearly as many degrees as a right angle (which has ninety)!

Most Christians—men and women in Christ—have never been on Mastermind or belonged to Mensa. Some may not have a very high IQ. Nevertheless all those "in Christ" are one of the

GOD'S ANSWER FOR PRESSURE

intelligentsia, for living "in Christ" means the divine bestowal of a wisdom that the world knows nothing about: "You are wise in Christ."

There is a great difference between wisdom and learning. Through the world's educational system we may acquire learning, but that does not make us wise. Many people who have acquired a great deal of learning do unwise things.

The secret of the Christian's wisdom, which allays the pressure of ignorance, is this: "The fear of the Lord is the beginning of wisdom." Life in Christ results in a full and satisfying life, both mentally as well as spiritually. Human learning or knowledge is *acquired* (through attendance at school, for example); but spiritual wisdom is *imparted*.

The Christian's wisdom is freely given by God, and it is given to all who are in Christ Jesus. No entrance examination has to be taken. No degrees have to be earned. There is no requirement for research resulting in a doctorate. Worldly learning often is gained through inducements: "We'll give you a new bike, Johnny, if you pass your exam." The pressure of, "You'll always be an ignorant pig unless you do well academically" is not for the Christian. The believer has put his trust in a living Savior and thus, has received "Christ the power of God, and the wisdom of God" (1 Corinthians 4:24). Christ is God's wisdom personified, and when you have the Person then you have the wisdom.

THE PRESSURE OF IGNORANCE

Of course, by worldly standards, the wise Christian still may be looked on as foolish and ignorant by those who possess mere "worldly wisdom." Our wisdom is "wisdom in Christ" and if we possess a B.A. degree then it stands for "Born Again." There was a theological college lecturer who was unable to fulfill a preaching engagement in a country church because of illness. He was a Doctor of Theology. Writing his apology to the church, he said he would be sending a mere student in his place, but he was afraid the student was not a Doctor in Theology. The church secretary replied saying, "That does not matter for our theology is not sick!"

D.L. Moody, the famous evangelist, was considered by some to be like the early disciples of Christ, "ignorant and unlearned men." But Moody was mightily used in Great Britain among the learned of Cambridge University.

God's wisdom is "spiritually discerned." It cannot be understood by a mere man of the world. Often it is understood by a simple of heart believer, one who is child-like, not child-ish. Such spiritual discernment is a gift of God's Holy Spirit. He opens the eyes and mind to an understanding of God's wisdom. Receiving it does not win the applause and adulation of men, but it does help to relieve us from the pressures, strains, and stresses of everyday living. It allows us to see the purposes of God and the plan of God for our lives. It enables us to see the

GOD'S ANSWER FOR PRESSURE

needs of our fellow men. It helps us every moment of the day and around every corner of life's road to rest in the knowledge that God knows, God loves, and God cares.

Are you ignorant at this very moment about the solution to some pressing problem? Do you find it difficult to cope with the pressures of problems like divorce, drug addiction, disease, or death? Do you feel ignorant about some personal problem that seems too embarrassing to talk to another about? Knowing that you ought to witness about Christ to unsaved friends, relatives, and workmates, yet feeling too ignorant about spiritual truths to make the first move, what can you do? A short prayer will soon provide the answer and the spiritual wisdom necessary for "giving a reason for the hope within you."

In our modern educational system there often is no allowance given for "the late developer." Young people are put into categories of intelligence right from an early age, and if they fall behind they are left with those of similar standards. No account is taken of Christian conversion and the resultant desire to make something of one's life for the same of Christ and His church. Many a minister and missionary can vouch for the truth of this. It was so in my own case.

Until the age of sixteen I was lazy at school and had no desire to "do well," as they used to put it. I remained in one class for several years instead of

THE PRESSURE OF IGNORANCE

moving up with others of the same age group. After conversion and a conviction that God was calling me to the Christian ministry I knew that certain standards would be required of me in order to enter the university and theological college. With God's help I quickly made up for lost time and caught up with those who had gone before. Examinations were passed, diplomas and degrees gained, not because I had suddenly become a brilliant student, but because I now wanted to bring honor and glory to the God who had saved me and wanted me to serve Him. Not being brilliant I had to become like William Carey who emphasized before his death that any future biographer must point out that he, too, was not brilliant but a "plodder." "I can plod" said Carey, and God used him as he has used many late developers and plodders since.

"Learn of Me," said Jesus. Yes, that is the secret to the solution of the problem of the pressure of ignorance. Living close to Him by being in Him, we learn of Him, through prayer, meditation, Bible study, and the fellowship of His people.

None is too ignorant or too old to learn Christ's wisdom. All we have to do is to pray the words of an old hymn:

> *Teach us, Lord, Thy wisdom,*
> *While we seek men's lore;*
> *May the mind be humbled*
> *As we know Thee more;*

GOD'S ANSWER FOR PRESSURE

Let the larger vision
Bring the childlike heart,
And our deeper knowledge
Holier zeal impart.
   Author unknown

Beyond the printed page, the Word of God as set forth in the Bible, is the spoken word. It is in the quietness of the Secret Place, communing with Christ through His Spirit, that He speaks to us and imparts His true wisdom.

Father, forgive us for those times when we have relied on our own understanding and have been guided by the wisdom that is in Christ. Open our spiritual ears and mind, filling us with divine knowledge that will enable us to cope with the pressures of ignorance, bringing release and gladness into our lives and the lives of others.

Chapter Fifteen

THE PRESSURE OF INSECURITY

He which stablisheth us with you in Christ . . . is God.

2 Corinthians 1:21

To accept Christ is to become a member of the "established" Church! This does not mean a certain section of the visible Church on earth. It means, having found Christ, accepted Him by faith, and then baptized into His mystical Body by the Holy Spirit, God establishes us in Christ. "Establishes" means that He puts us on a firm footing or stabilizes us. An ocean-going liner has stabilizers fitted so that in stormy weather the pitch and roll of the vessel is lessened. This results in more comfort for passengers, less chance of sea-sickness, and less loss of dishes owing to breakage through sliding off the tables.

New converts to Christ need spiritual stabilizers.

GOD'S ANSWER FOR PRESSURE

Certainly they should do as their spiritual counselors have urged them: join a church where they will hear faithful Bible teaching and enjoy choice fellowship among the Lord's people. Certainly they should read their Bibles and pray regularly in the quietness of their own homes. But that does not always make for an established Christian.

A busy-body went to D.L. Moody and said, "Mr. Moody, I saw one of your converts drunk in the gutter last night." Moody replied: "Yes, that must have been one of my converts; if he had been one of God's then it would not have been so!" Are you a Moody convert, a Billy Graham convert, another preacher's convert, or one of God's converts? If your finding and accepting Christ has been the result of the Holy Spirit's work in you then you are one of God's converts and He who has begun a good work in you will finish it; He will establish you in Christ.

There is no other way of facing up to the trials, persecutions, afflictions, temptations, and adversity. All those and other situations and circumstances that make us feel so insecure, can only be counteracted by being stabilized in Christ. When we feel insecure through friends letting us down, or because our wage packet seems inadequate to meet all the bills, or our meager pension causes us to adopt a rather frugal and unaccustomed lifestyle, then it is we need to be sure of God's establishing us in Christ.

THE PRESSURE OF INSECURITY

Daren was brought up in a very difficult home and suffered much insecurity as a result. Whenever he came with a party of young people from the church to our home we could see him stealthily pocketing biscuits, cakes, sandwiches to take home with him. He already had eaten more than anyone else in the room so I often wondered if he ate all these "extras" when he got home to his bedroom.

When visiting his home he always brought out a box of what he called "my treasures" to show me. Usually it was a discarded tin box or cardboard shoe box. It was filled with odd scraps like an old bus ticket, a matchbox, a picture postcard or some metal object he might have found along the railway line on one of his walks.

If brother or sister came into the room while he was showing me these "treasures" he would quickly put the lid on the box and take it back to his bedroom. He became "an enquirer" many times over, but only to receive counseling literature which he could add to his collection of treasures. He made a profession of faith in Christ over and over again, but his nominal Christian parents did nothing in the home to underline what he had been told about Christianity in Sunday School, youth group, and church.

It was no wonder that when the time came to leave school (and his dayschool teachers had been unable to cope with his great insecurity) he joined a branch of the armed forces. The army, navy, or air force, engender a sense of belonging to a family. The discipline he experienced was just right for one who had been brought up in a home where mother and father pulled in opposite directions. He knew where he was in the army and so felt secure with officers and men surrounding him. For the first time in his life the pressure of insecurity was lightened and he was living an established life.

The relief from insecurity through God's establishing us in Christ was a choice truth for Paul. He used two figures of speech to describe it. Believers who were established were either "sealed" or "anointed."

Anointing was an illustration from royalty. Kings were anointed at their coronation. For Paul, being established was like being inducted into a royal family. Now a king does not feel insecure for he has position, power, and wealth. He wants for nothing. His life is guarded by soldiers and he is guided by wise counselors.

Sealing was an illustration from the legal profession. Documents, deeds, contracts, and covenants are sealed as a sign of genuineness and authenticity. Sealing also is a mark of ownership. In Paul's day timber would bear a seal before being floated down a river to the sea, sealed with the mark of the owner.

Just as royalty does not experience insecurity, neither does a property owner. He has a deed saying that the property is his. A tenant may feel

THE PRESSURE OF INSECURITY

insecure, for his landlord may seek his eviction. The "squatter" feels insecure, for he knows he has no right to be there. The Christian, then, is like the property owner. Our bodies are temples of the Holy Spirit. We are "anointed" and "sealed." Christ lives in us and we live in Him. God has established us.

In Christ then we cannot be moved or swayed by the pressures of insecurity. To move us Christ must be moved. If we are to waver or falter then Christ must be unsteady. But He is unwavering, steadfast, the living, incarnate "Amen," the One who ratifies every promise of God.

We need not falter or fail in our Christian faith. We need not grow weary in Christian service. We can remain steadfast in the faith because we have been established in Christ.

In 1985 a British marine sailed out to Rockall, a very isolated rock in the Atlantic Ocean off the coast of Scotland. Using climbing gear he not only scaled this barren rock but pitched a tent and stayed there for one month. At times he was in danger of being swept into the sea. Unfurling a Union Jack he claimed the rock as British Territory, although it has no inherent importance for military reasons. He was hailed as a hero when he was lifted off the rock for it had been quite a feat of endurance to stay for so long on such an exposed site. When asked, "Didn't you shake with fright when the seas and winds were high?" He replied, "Yes, I did, but the rock didn't!"

GOD'S ANSWER FOR PRESSURE

The believer in Christ lives on a rock, Christ Jesus, and "other foundation can no man lay than that which is laid, Jesus Christ." God has lifted the pressure of insecurity and placed our feet on an impregnable rock. He has established us for all time and eternity.

Heavenly Father, before I undertake the duties of this day, knowing the insecure world in which I live, keep me mindful of my standing in Christ. May the constancy and consistency of my life be a benediction to those with whom I come into contact.

Chapter Sixteen

THE PRESSURE OF INCONSTANCY

_____ [write your own name on the blank line], approved in Christ.

Romans 16:10

Have you written your name on the line above? Perhaps you couldn't because you do not fully understand what "approved" means. Well, if you are living in Christ, then you are to be "of good reputation after trial," for that is what "approved" means.

Apelles, to whom Paul is referring in Romans 6:10, had been tried, tested, and found faithful. In the same way you and I are to "study to show [ourselves] approved by God." We are to "study," that is, strive hard at, work at it, make it our daily business to become "approved in Christ."

Sometimes as a retired Pastor (after thirty-six years in the Christian ministry), I am asked by

GOD'S ANSWER FOR PRESSURE

young ministers: "What do you think is the main difference in our churches today from when you began?" I can answer without hesitation, "The lack of commitment; the loss of constancy among the membership." Even twenty years ago you could rely on church members to undertake some form of Christian work or service and carry it through to the bitter end, perhaps devoting a lifetime to it. Today many Christians begin some form of Christian work and then give it up within a few weeks or months. Their only excuse often is, "For personal reasons!" It would not have done for John Bunyan, as he wrote in his famous hymn:

> *One here will constant be,*
> *Come wind, come weather.*

As a young man I was greatly influenced by the Scripture Union's children's evangelist, R. Hudson Pope. Hudson Pope wrote many choruses, a fine book about children's work, *To Teach Others Also*, and conducted a multitude of children's missions, in church halls and especially on the beaches of summer resorts along the coastline of Great Britain. And he did this until he was over eighty years of age! One of the prominent leaders of the Scripture Union once confided in me and said, "We can't get young men who will devote a lifetime to this work any more; two, three, or five years and then they give it up for something else." Hudson Pope was not one to give in to the pressure of inconstancy and

THE PRESSURE OF INCONSTANCY

thus successive generations of men like myself learned how to conduct children's meetings, how to give talks to children with effective visual aids, and how to "draw in the net" at the close of the meetings and counsel the young enquirers.

Hudson Pope kept an old seaman's-type "tin" chest. At his death it was found to be filled with letters written to him by his child converts. Many of these were from boys who later entered the Christian ministry and became very well-known preachers, gracing the Keswick Convention platform, for instance. Yet those of us who had the privilege of providing hospitality for Hudson Pope during a week or ten day's mission soon learned of the personal trials and griefs which he patiently bore. He was constant, and he was "approved" or found to be of good reputation after trial.

Do you feel like shouting "Glory, hallelujah!" on Sunday in church and then "Why are you cast down, O my soul?" on Monday morning when the world exerts its pressures to make you inconstant? That is surely not the attitude of one living a life in Christ.

King Nebuchadnezzar put three men in a fiery furnace. But they were not only in a furnace, they were in Christ, and Christ (the preexistent Christ) was in the furnace with them. The king had to confess: "I see four men loose . . . and the form of the fourth is like the Son of God." It was Christ who gave them courage and constancy,

GOD'S ANSWER FOR PRESSURE

endurance, and victory. They came out of the furnace "approved."

Our fiery trials may very well be like a furnace—hot, unbearable, uncomfortable, restrictive. There is nothing like the pressure of suffering, pain, anguish, bewilderment, to make us inconstant. But in Christ it can be borne patiently, courageously, and victoriously.

An advertisement for a Christian holiday home read like this: "Good fellowship—separate tables—constant hot water!" The separate tables cancelled out the fellowship. And the constant hot water? Well, that describes the life of many of us. We are constantly being burned, scorched, singed by sickness, affliction, trial, testing, or persecution. But we can come through it all "approved in Christ."

Living in Christ means that the help of Christ is available to us in the secular as well as the sacred realm. Soon the secular becomes spiritual and the spiritual becomes sacred. We find that we perform our secular tasks "as unto the Lord" and our Christian service is done in order that we might make the world a better place.

Of course, others may not approve of us. They may find every opportunity to show their disapproval. It may be that our Christian witness or the conscientious way we carry out our daily work is like a straight stick laid alongside a crooked one. The Christian's life shows up the deficiencies of the unbeliever's way of living and so they disapprove.

THE PRESSURE OF INCONSTANCY

Does it matter? Can we not say with the hymnwriter: "The Master praises, what are men?"

The world may ask us, "What are you worth?" or "How far up the ladder of success have you got?" In their eyes we may not be influential or successful, but success for the Christian is being counted one of those "approved in Christ."

Not all of us can be Phoebes (see Romans 16), carriers of important theological, apostolic epistles. Not all of us can be Aquillas and Priscillas, using our homes for Christian hospitality and worship. Few of us can be like Andronicus and Junia, "of note among the apostles." But we can all be like Apelles, "approved in Christ."

What of the suffering when we do not succumb to the pressure of inconstancy? We shall come out of it, like Job, "tried as gold," having on us the hallmark of genuineness, our Savior's approval. The suffering will still be hard to bear, but learning that we are "partaker(s) of Christ's sufferings" we shall discover a rich and deep fellowship with Him. We shall cease to rebel against suffering and our experience will be:

When through fiery trials thy pathway shall lie,
My grace all-sufficient shall be thy supply;
The flame shall not hurt thee; I only design
Thy dross to consume, and thy gold to refine.
George Keith or "K"
in Rippon's *Selection,* 1787

GOD'S ANSWER FOR PRESSURE

At first we may be tempted to say, "This is one experience I can well do without," and so we try to run away, or resist, or rebel. If we do we shall miss the experience of the "fellowship of His sufferings" and therefore the stamp of His approval when it is all over. It will all make sense one day when we look back and see how God was in the trial and trouble with us, even though we look back through tears. Sometimes we shall not even see it like that but shall have to wait for the explanation to be given us in what Spurgeon called "the fair schoolroom of the sky." From such a heavenly vantage point we shall see and understand it all and confess that "He does all things well."

Now can you write your name on the blank line?

Help us, O Lord, to bear our trials patiently. Help us to enter into the trials of others, giving them support and sympathy. Accept our thanks for past deliverances and strengthen us for all that is to come. So may we serve You with constancy as well as courage.

Chapter Seventeen

THE PRESSURE OF INADEQUACY

> If there be therefore any consolation in Christ.
>
> Philippians 2:1

Living in Christ is not an insurance policy for living an easy life and facing a rosy future. Conversion does not result automatically in freedom from the pressures of life. The world will still deliver hard knocks and down we will go, sometimes flat on our face. When we do go under, however, as God's children in Christ, we shall always have the "consolation in Christ" to soften the blow and strengthen us for getting up again.

Often we face the pressure of inadequacy. Our old jalopy of a car is seen to be inadequate for modern traffic congestion and road conditions. It just hasn't got the necessary acceleration any more. As the chilldren grow up our house becomes inadequate and an extension has to be built. But these material inadequacies can all be met by material means. By taking a bank loan, increasing the mortgage on our home, these and other contingency plans enable us to cope.

By contrast it is not so easy to cope with the pressure of mental, moral, or spiritual inadequacies. Inadequacies of character, mental ability, and spirituality are a different kettle of fish. But God has a contingency plan for such inadequacies—"consolation in Christ."

A man in the New Testament was called "Son of Consolation." His real name was Barnabas. Praise God that Barnabases are not confined to the New Testament. Many of us are thankful to sons and daughters of consolation in our own generation. Within the bounds of the Christian church we often have become indebted to consolers of others.

There is a limit, however, to the consolation that one person can give another. We discover this especially at times of bereavement. How inadequate we feel when trying to comfort a friend or relative whose loved one has died. We can offer sympathy and comfort just so far and no further. At that point the only way to relieve the pressure of inadequacy is to commend the one we are trying to help to "the God of all comfort," the "God of patience and consolation," whose comfort is "everlasting consolation."

THE PRESSURE OF INADEQUACY

I began preaching as a "boy preacher" of sixteen, first accompanying my father on his preaching engagements around the villege "Bethels" of "happy, hearty, healthy Hertfordshire" (Charles Lamb). Fortunately I have kept a record of my early sermon notes. I am simply astounded at my audacity! Sermons on pain, suffering and death, as well as direct evangelistic gospel messages. What did a boy of sixteen know of pain and suffering? My upbringing at home and school was extremely happy. I do not remember any serious illnesses or the loss of near relatives or friends. How dare I preach outside my experience? Well, my father taught me to do as C.H. Spurgeon did and preach "a full-orbed gospel" or as Paul would say, "the whole counsel of God." So as best as I was able I preached from Scripture and expounded such subjects as pain and suffering.

Some forty to fifty years later I heard from a very old man that he still remembered a sermon I had preached on "Watchman, what of the night?" At the time I preached it the Second World War was imminent and it appears it had ministered to his heart and to others in the congregation who were very depressed, most of them having already experienced the First World War. What a blessing I did not succumb to the pressure of inadequacy as a young teenager and so neglect in my preaching doctrines that were outside my experience.

What consolation there is for the man or woman who is in Christ! Paul is not using the word "if" in

GOD'S ANSWER FOR PRESSURE

the sense of doubt or uncertainty. It is his way of urging us to seek out and acquire the consolation that is being freely offered. In Christ there is sufficient consolation for us all, however tried, sorrowful, lonely or downcast we might be. While others may try to console us, and how thankful we are for their efforts, Christ Himself is consolation personified. By living in Him it is available at all times, near at hand, for this consolation is within us.

There is no grief or distress that is beyond the all-powerful and everlasting Consoler who lives within the Christian's innermost being. Learn to live more closely in Him and the nearer will be His consolation when you need it most.

But the consolation that is in Christ is only one side of the coin. Paul is urging the Christians at Philippi to console one another. By virtue of being a Christ-person you have a source of consolation within which you can impart to others whatever your feelings of inadequacy might be. Sometimes this is called "switching on the sunshine." So many people today live in the grip of winter. A black thunder cloud seems constantly above their heads. Wintertime is in their soul. You can "switch on the sunshine" and help someone like that. By sharing the consolation that is in Christ with such a person you can bring them out of winter into summer sunshine.

Do you know summertime in the soul, even when it's wintertime in the world around you? Can you sing daily, because you are in Christ:

THE PRESSURE OF INADEQUACY

There is sunshine in my soul to-day
More glorious and bright
Than glows in any earthly sky;
For Jesus is my light.

There is springtime in my soul to-day,
For when the Lord is near,
The dove of peace sings in my heart,
The flowers of grace appear.
                               E.E. Hewitt

This has nothing to do with what psychologists call your "general condition" or your "natural disposition." Because you yourself are feeling "under the weather" or "below par" that does not mean you cannot help someone else. Sometimes it is the depressed who can best help the depressed. "It takes one to know one" says the sufferer. In the same way our Lord, "a man of sorrows and acquainted with grief," could console others.

Every town and city, village and hamlet, has someone who has been hurt, someone to whom life has been cruel, people upon whom the world has pressed heavily. Let us who are in Christ be sensitive to their needs and sensitive to the consoling presence of Christ within us. This cannot be learned from books, only through experience. This is one of the rich results of being in Christ—we have a built-in sensitivity about the needs of others, and awareness that we can be channels through whom Christ's consolation flows to others. We become "touched with a feeling of their infirmity" and our quickened eye, coupled with a gentle hand and soft-spoken word provides the consolation they are desperately yearning for—consolation in Christ.

Lift us up to You, O Lord God, that we may see Your greatness and gain comfort from it. Help us to see something of the great heart of compassion our Savior had and his tender way with men and women when on earth. When human consolation reaches its limit, take over from us and comfort and bless those we are trying to help.

Chapter Eighteen

THE PRESSURE OF INFLUENCES

> Ye have ten thousand instructors in Christ.
>
> 1 Corinthians 4:15

How did you find Christ? Was it through the witness of another? That "another" Paul calls an "instructor" or tutor. He himself was such a tutor and so became the spiritual father of the many who found Christ through his ministry.

It may not have been just one person who helped you to find Christ. Paul writes of "ten thousand instructors." Maybe he did use exaggerated language but it was designed to impress upon us our indebtedness to those who showed us how to find Christ.

Did you have a godly mother and father? Who taught you to kneel by your bed at night and pray? Who sung you to sleep with a child's hymn? Who taught you the importance and delight of worship in God's house of prayer on the Lord's Day?

Perhaps it was a succession of Sunday School teachers who influenced you in spiritual things, or the leader of a Bible class. Perhaps that saintly old pastor was one of the "ten thousand" who led you to Christ for salvation. Maybe it was some unknown tract distributor.

In my case it was an elder brother who was converted at a Bible class camp and came home a changed boy. Why, he even began helping my mother with the washing-up of dirty dishes, without being asked to do so. And when he later started work he gave me weekly pocket money. That proved to me the reality of his faith!

Often it is a missionary on furlough whose exciting stories of God's work overseas stirs some young heart towards belief in Christ. And since God used "even the wrath of man" to praise him, and ungodly leaders like Cyrus to work out His purposes, what of that atheistic schoolteacher? Did he or she not rather send you nearer to the truth in Christ instead of turning you against it? Remember that one of the greatest defenses of the resurrection of Christ is in the book *Who Moved the Stone?*—and the author first of all set out to disprove the resurrection!

This list of some of the possible "ten thousand instructors" could be extended over and over again. And often it was not their logic, rhetoric, charming

THE PRESSURE OF INFLUENCES

personality, or academic qualifications that equipped them for their personal ministry to you, it was simply because they were in Christ. Living daily in His presence, knowing the Savior intimately, walking with Him moment by moment, the result is that others could see Christ in you.

In my case it was a Bible class leader who called at my home every Sunday and walked with me to the class. He didn't preach at me but I could see Jesus in him. He gave me an old typewriter (it still worked) and an instruction manual. I used it for many years, being too poor in the ministry to buy a better one, and my first books were written on it. But it was not the gift that drew me to that man, it was his interest in all that I did: schoolwork, sport, hobbies, and so on. But above all it was his fine Christian character.

Such an influence was needed to counteract the pressure of other influences at work upon a teenager. The temptations to be found in the English public school system in those days can be read about in old novels like *Tom Brown's Schooldays*. Today they seem mild by the comparison with the evil influences of these modern times. Today's school boy or girl and college students have to beware of the influences of television, vulgar movies (dealing with the horrors of homosexuality, lesbianism, and blood-and-guts violence), drug addiction, pornography, and the occult, among other horrors.

GOD'S ANSWER FOR PRESSURE

Christian parents can guard against some of these evil influences coming into their homes, but they cannot stop their children coming into contact with them in the homes of their friends and acquaintances.

My son, besides being a Baptist pastor also is chaplain to a mixed college. Frequently he is asked to speak about television programs and give the Christian's view of them. He finds that the soap operas are having a terrifying effect on the minds of young people. Infidelity and divorce is the accepted thing. In most "soaps" people are in and out of bed with one another at the slightest excuse. Where the solution to a problem used to be a cigarette or a drink, it is now a brazen request (often made by the woman rather than the man) to "Stay the night and make love to me."

Not only do these evil influences make it difficult for the non-Christian to find Christ, they also bring pressure to bear on the young Christian who should be "following on to know the Lord." I frequently have been asked to see that a Sunday night service is concluded by a certain time, "otherwise we shall miss the latest episode of our favorite TV show." If this is not done then they are likely to walk out before the service is over. In the same way midweek prayer meetings and Bible studies suffer from non-attenders because of the attraction of television. No wonder it often is referred to as "the one-eyed giant." It is a giant that

THE PRESSURE OF INFLUENCES

dominates the lives of many and often has Christians in its grip.

It is only those who are truly in Christ who can be one of the "ten thousand instructors" encouraging others to break free from the giant's power. In Paul's day a tutor or pedagogue was usually a slave. He was a strict tutor for he knew that if he failed in his job his master would punish him. Sometimes, then, instructors have to be cruel to be kind. The preacher has to "admonish" his congregation as well as encourage them. In love he has to warn and exhort and point out the evil influences that are at work in our society today.

Looking back to our own salvation, and the good influences that were at work to bring it about, we have to "teach others also" (as Paul wrote to Timothy) so that the pressure of bad influences is destroyed by the gospel message, which is "powerful to the pulling down of strongholds."

We may not be prominent, well-known preachers. We may only seem to be a small cog in the colossal machinery of God's eternal purposes. But, to change the figure of speech to a Pauline one, we can sow the seed and leave it to another to water it and let God give the increase. We may not even have to say a word. Often the life counts more than words from our lips. Being in Christ we can witness for Him in prominent places and in dark, obscure corners, unobserved and unnoticed. It is difficult to describe a sunset, and to photograph it properly, a filter will have to be used. Even then the colors may be inaccurate. A sunset has to be seen and experienced firsthand. It speaks for itself as we gaze at it and are captivated by it.

> *So let our lips and lives express*
> *The holy gospel we profess;*
> *So let our works and virtues shine,*
> *To prove the doctrine all divine.*
>
>   Isaac Watts

"*Father of mercies, bow Thine ear; Attentive to our earnest prayer: We plead for those who plead for Thee; Successful pleaders may they be.*

Teach them to sow the precious seed, Teach them Thy chosen flock to feed; Teach them immortal souls to gain, Souls that will well reward their pain."

                                    Benjamin Beddome

Chapter Nineteen

THE PRESSURE OF INSENSITIVITY

Love which is in Christ Jesus.
2 Timothy 1:13

The Christian Brethren have a "morning meeting" on the Lord's Day which is described as "Worship and the Breaking of Bread." Believing that the priesthood of believers is best manifested in this meeting, and not holding with a "one man ministry," all can take part in this meeting or service as led by the Spirit.

The long-standing member of a Christian Brethren meeting knows that such a service needs great sensitivity on the part of those attending it. In a service conducted largely by one man, be he pastor, minister, vicar, or rector, only one person can make a mistake. When everyone present can take part then there can be many mistakes made, with resulting chaos and confusion.

GOD'S ANSWER FOR PRESSURE

In a Brethren morning meeting therefore there has to be sensitivity to the needs of others in worship. Where there is insensitivity the worship suffers. Others present can be offended by the one feeling led to speak, pray, or announce a Bible reading or a hymn. In a modern charismatic meeting there is even more sensitivity needed. Unlike most Brethren Assemblies the charismatic churches (often house churches) allow women as well as men to take part. They often allow dancing as well as tongues, interpretations, prophecies, and so on. Just as a spoken word can offend other worshipers, so can dancing, or praying or singing in tongues. "No man lives for himself" says Scripture, so we must be sensitive to the needs of others in worship as well as in day to day contact.

The secret of this sensitivity is love. But it must be love "which is in Christ Jesus." Now Paul always found it difficult to describe or define Christ's love. Because of its four dimensional nature, its length and breadth, height and depth, he wrote to the Ephesians saying that it was "incomprehensible." At best, all he could say was, that without love anything was nothing, and out of faith, hope, and love, love is the greatest of all.

The love Paul wrote about is no mere sentimental, emotional feeling. It is nothing like the so-called love depicted in the films of the 30s and 40s or the sexual lust of the twentieth century television soap operas. It is certainly not a weak emotion. The love of Christ

THE PRESSURE OF INSENSITIVITY

is strong, enabling us to "bear all things, believe all things, hope all things, and endure all things," even when under severe pressure. It never fails. How can it, for Christ never fails.

It is this kind of love that makes a marriage. Great sensitivity is needed for a happy marriage. Most divorces are the result of insensitivity. Either the man is insensitive of the woman's needs or *vice versa*. Insensitivity thus breeds resentment in one partner or both and so the couple grow apart.

It is also the kind of love that makes the Christian life and witness a wonderful testimony to the world. The early Christians were characterized by it for a Roman historian commented: "See how these Christians love one another." The sheer miracle of the "in Christ" partnership expresses itself day by day in love for God, Christ, the Holy Spirit, and one another.

Needless to say, this kind of love cannot be worked up, it must come from within. When, like Solomon we can say, "my beloved is mine and I am his," and really mean that Jesus is dearer and nearer to us than all the world and all the people in it, then we are beginning to experience this "love which is in Christ Jesus."

So we experience this love, and express this love, only according to the extent of Christ's occupancy of our lives. As we allow Him to permeate our whole being then His love is "shed abroad in our hearts by the Holy Spirit." We then begin to love ourselves as we ought, and also our neighbors.

A story is told of three churches of different denominations, all situated in the same street in close proximity to one another. As one congregation sang, "Will there be any stars in my crown?" another began to sing, "no, not one, no, not one!" The third congregation struck up the hymn, "Oh, that will be glory for me!" Perhaps there is more truth in the story of the man who prayed in the church prayer meeting, "Lord, send a revival, but to our church, not the Methodists down the road!" Real "love in Christ" prevents all such rivalry and competition.

Rivalry is seen among Christian ministers and clergy; there is competition between church officers (perhaps deacons or elders); and sometimes Sunday School teachers and Bible class leaders vie with one another to obtain the "pre-eminence" that Diotrophes coveted.

Discord and disharmony not only occur in a church when wrong notes are played by the organist but when human "instruments" are out of tune. We become out of tune when we are out of step with the Lord of love.

What a supernatural quality there is about this "love which is in Christ Jesus." It is not natural to love everybody else. Other people have such off-putting quirks or traits of character, and they offend us by their outrageous conduct, that we find it hard

THE PRESSURE OF INSENSITIVITY

to like them, let alone love them. Some grate on us. Some just seem unloveable. But Jesus loves them all, so it is possible for us to do so if we are filled with His supernatural love.

Since it is supernatural Paul is quite right in saying that it is incomprehensible and indescribable. Who can define a sunset? It is difficult to describe one, let alone define one. A beautiful evening sky is a chemistry of colors. Not even a brilliant artist or a superb color film can do justice to it. So with Christ's love. It comes down from above, from the Father in heaven. It fills the believer in his innermost being. It flows out to others. It moves our heart, our mind, our soul, and our will. It controls us emotionally, intellectually, spiritually, and volitionally.

Yes, Jesus can not only live His lovely life through us, but also His limitless love. We not only live as one with Him, we love as one with Him. That makes us nicer people to know. That relieves the pressure of insensitivity and helps us to be sensitive to the needs of others. As this love comes in, it drives out all hatred, jealousy, resentment, rivalry, and unloveliness. As these are driven out, more and more room is left to be filled with divine love.

No longer do we have to try hard to love people. We just let the Lord love them through us. Instead of being insensitive to their needs and reacting against their "bad" points (usually we react against the very thing or things that is marring our own character!) we begin to love them as Christ loves them. His love enabled Him to leave heaven, come to earth, suffer, and die on the cross for our sakes. Only daily union, through being in Christ, can bring about a love life that truly is satisfying, rewarding, and a witness to the transforming power of the gospel.

> *Love divine, all loves excelling,*
> *Joy of heaven, to earth come down,*
> *Fix in us thy humble dwelling,*
> *All thy faithful mercies crown:*
> *Jesus, thou art all compassion,*
> *Pure, unbounded love thou art;*
> *Visit us with thy salvation,*
> *Enter every trembling heart.*
> Charles Wesley

Chapter Twenty

THE PRESSURE OF IMMATURITY

> Every man perfect in Christ Jesus.
> Colossians 1:28

As you live *in Christ* daily do you wish sometimes you were more Christlike? Do you not wish you had made more strides in the Christian life? Do you not hope that one day there will be fewer cracks in your Christian character and fewer chinks in your spiritual armor?

Most of us must have said at some time or other (when excusing our conduct): "Well, nobody's perfect, are they?" No, we're not, even though some misguided exponents of holiness or a "higher life" movement might have talked about "sinless perfection." We know from experience, as well as from the writings of the apostle Paul, that the life in Christ is a "fight to be fought and a race to be run." Daily living in Christ does not excuse us from daily

GOD'S ANSWER FOR PRESSURE

battle with Satan and the powers of darkness. It is a life and death battle and a marathon of a race.

So what does Paul mean when he says "Every man perfect in Christ Jesus?" Perfect means fully grown or mature.

What a pitiful sight it is to see an adult who has never grown up—to see a grown man or woman still dressing, speaking, giggling, and generally behaving like a child or teenager! "Empty-headed" is the scornful epithet often used of such a person. And it is not only outward signs of immaturity such as dress and speech; it also is the moods and sulks of a schoolboy or schoolgirl that characterize the immature adult—moodiness or sulkiness in order to get one's own way.

It is possible to be spiritually empty-headed. Having found life in Christ, the new convert fails to grow up into Christ in all things, longing for spiritual maturity. Even young Christians, young in years, should desire to become spiritually grownup. The apostle John gives us the scriptural pattern in his letter when he writes to "children . . . young men . . . fathers."

In Scripture, the number seven is considered the number of completion or perfection. There are seven steps to maturity, counteracting the pressure of immaturity, the state of stunted growth that Satan wishes to see. First, there must be *good daily food*. No baby grows up without a healthy, nutritious, balanced diet, augmented by vitamins and minerals

THE PRESSURE OF IMMATURITY

if necessary. Well, God's Word is milk, meat, and honey, our "necessary food." Without reading it regularly, studying it diligently, absorbing it, and being absorbed by it, and meditating on it, we shall never grow into mature believers.

Next, step two is *fresh air*. The baby is taken out in the baby carriage, thus benefitting from fresh air and sunshine. Oxygen must be breathed in if the baby is to develop lung power. With insufficient oxygen we tend to faint and become dizzy. Prayer has been described by James Montgomery as "the Christian's vital breath." Without prayer we die spiritually.

The third requirement is *exercise*. The baby begins with a baby bouncer on the door lintel, or some other form of exercise that will gradually strengthen weak limbs and so give mobility and sturdiness. Later on, at school, certain sports will again help to produce a fit, healthy, and well-developed child. Today aerobics and jogging are being recommended to those quite old in years, in order to keep the heart in healthy shape. Christian service is the Christian's spiritual exercise. No believer who is living in Christ should consider sitting in an armchair with house slippers on. Such "taking one's ease in Zion" is no way to maturity. There is a whole lost world that needs to be told the Good News of eternal life in Christ.

Rest is the fourth step towards spiritual maturity. Sleep is important for the growing child. Television

GOD'S ANSWER FOR PRESSURE

must not be watched until late at night when the child needs plenty of rest and sleep to prepare for school the next day. This rest for the believer is reliance on God at all times in simple faith. J.S. Pigott expressed it well when she wrote:

> *Ever lift Thy face upon me,*
> *As I work and wait for Thee;*
> *Resting 'neath Thy smile, Lord Jesus,*
> *Earth's dark shadows flee.*
> *Brightness of my Father's glory,*
> *Sunshine of my Father's face,*
> *Keep me ever trusting, resting:*
> *Fill me with Thy grace.*

Step five is a *clean environment*. There has been one experiment of bringing up a baby through childhood to teenage years keeping him free from contamination in a "glass bubble," but not every small child can be so fully protected. Parents, do, however, try to guard their children from infection and contamination. Homes, clothes, and food—these are kept clean or prepared under hygenic conditions. So the child of God must stay away from places where sin might soil the soul. Holiness and separation are necessary for the spiritual maturity of the believer.

Step number six is *loving care*. A child may be given a good home (or rather a fine house) to live in, and be surrounded by a great variety of toys. He may have good, wholesome, well-cooked food. But

THE PRESSURE OF IMMATURITY

if there is no love and concern, then the house remains a building of bricks and mortar and does not become a home in which he or she can become mature. So the believer needs to frequent God's "house" and grow to maturity among God's family.

Finally, step number seven, is that of *regular check-ups*. The doctor, the dentist, and optician all need to be visited at regular intervals to see if the child is growing up without defects. Heart, lungs, teeth, eyes, ears—all these and more need constant checking to see that no disease is developing. So the believer must learn to take his spiritual pulse, gauge the condition of his heart (examining it for unconfessed sin), and see that ears and eyes are only hearing and seeing those things which will enhance the spiritual condition.

Thus will the believer "grow in grace and in the knowledge of our Lord and Savior, Jesus Christ" (2 Peter 3:18).

Such a man or woman in Christ is so mature that he is not at the mercy of the representatives of the false sects and cults. He is able to say, "I know whom I have believed" and not only *whom* but "I know *what* I believe." The mature Christian is not at the mercy of the proponents of "isms" or *new* theology or *new* morality. He knows where he stands, where he is going, and what to say and do in defense of "the faith once and for all delivered to the saints."

GOD'S ANSWER FOR PRESSURE

On to maturity then. No more being "tossed to and fro." Physical growth is not through self-effort. So with spiritual growth. It is letting the life of Christ fill us completely.

Look in a mirror to see if you are putting on weight (if the tightness of your trousers does not already tell you). Listen, if you are a child, to comments like "My, how you've grown" to know if you have grown taller. Look into the mirror of God's Word to tell if you have grown more mature since the day of your conversion.

O Lord, illumine and stir my mind that I may become a more mature disciple of Your dear Son. No matter what pressures there are from without to keep me underdeveloped, make me conscious of your Spirit of grace and growth within, making me a radiant witness to Christ in my life.

Chapter Twenty-One

THE PRESSURE OF IRRELEVANCY

>Every good thing which is in you in Christ Jesus.
>
>Philemon 1:5

We live in a world of big problems: drugs, drink, divorce, violence, vandalism, sexually transmitted diseases, and so on. Yet most people's lives are concerned, by contrast, with irrelevancies.

Often these irrelevancies or "pin-pricks" take up more of our time (and sometimes money) than bigger, more important issues.

As a preacher, as well as an author, I can say that pastors and preachers usually are surrounded by irrelevancies. Only recently I was preaching in a church and had used, as I often do, visual aids. On one of my pictures I had painted a star. Shaking hands at the door with the congregation after the service a young man in his twenties commented,

GOD'S ANSWER FOR PRESSURE

"Your star only had five points, it should have had six!" He had completely missed the message I had delivered on the text, "So if the Son shall make you free you shall be free indeed" (John 8:36). My star, by the way had been irrelevant—I had only used it as a fill-in in a blank corner of my flash card. But his comment was even more irrelevant.

Irrelevant comments to preachers. Irrelevant condemnatory remarks to evangelists, politicians, and others. Irrelevant symptoms described to psychiatrists, given merely to mask a deep, inner hurt. So we could go on. We live most of the day beneath the pressure of irrelevancy.

Sometimes our faith is irrelevant to life. We become so concerned with minor points of doctrine that we forget the unsaved world around us in need of the doctrine of eternal salvation. Yes, there are still those who nit-pick over pre-, post-, or amillennialism, whether Christ will return to earth before or after the millennium or whether there will not be a millennium at all. Better by far to be a pan-millennialist, believing that everything will "pan out" all right since God is working His purpose out "as year succeeds to year!"

Does our faith only affect ourselves? Does it fail to affect the lives of others? Then perhaps we are living under the pressure of irrelevancies.

Paul did not succumb to irrelevancies. Even a cursory reading of Romans, Galatians, or Colossians reveals that Paul dealt with the big, momentous

THE PRESSURE OF IRRELEVANCY

things of our faith. Even when writing a personal letter to Philemon on behalf of a recaptured, runaway slave, he kept away from irrelevancies. He could have written about such things as "How much did Onesimus steal from you?" Or he could have asked, "How much out of pocket are you through buying a replacement slave?" He could have suggested that Onesimus should be reinstated but at a lower rung on the ladder. But no. He writes to Philemon in brotherly terms, reminding him of "every good thing which is in you in Christ."

Paul was stressing that because Philemon was in Christ, everything good about Philemon, goodness of character and goodness of conduct, was due to his being in Christ. The world maintains that "there is a little bit of bad in the best of us, and a little bit of good in the worst of us." The Christian knows that his little bit of good is all of God's grace and Christ's salvation. Our goodness is not our means of salvation for we are saved by faith, through grace, not by our good works. Our good works are the *fruit* and not the *root* of our salvation. Our good works are to the practical exhibition of our faith, the faith that imparted goodness to our characters.

The old black preacher put it: "Brethren, we have a believing and a behaving side to our faith." That is, our good works do not save us, but our belief in Christ does. The result of that belief in Christ means we then behave in a truly Christian way, "doing

GOD'S ANSWER FOR PRESSURE

good to all men, especially to those of the household of faith [God's family]."

It was to Philemon's "behaving side" that Paul was appealing. Forgetting irrelevancies, the apostle appealed to the heart of the matter, Philemon's heart that had been renewed through his faith in Jesus Christ.

"I know your works" said our Lord to one of the seven churches of Asia. And He knows ours. And Paul knew Philemon's. Do our Christian friends know them too?

I have seen churches split and divided by such irrelevancies as the pulpit rail painted or stained a wrong color. Or, whether the minister should be gowned or robed. Or, whether the vesper should be the same every Sunday night or the minister of music should choose a different one. The list is endless! These and many more irrelevancies have caused heated arguments in church meetings, among deacons' and finance committees. And all the time there are needy people and needy causes waiting for our good works.

The word good, we should remember, does not occur in the dictionary until after God. So our good works should follow our commitment to God's Son as Savior and Lord. Humanly speaking we have to say, "In me dwells no good thing." Spiritually speaking, because we are in Christ, there is "every good thing" in us as well as in Philemon.

It is a spiritual law that the deeper we dwell in

THE PRESSURE OF IRRELEVANCY

Christ the higher we rise spiritually. The more we rest in Him, the busier we want to become for Him. The more we receive from Him the more we are able to offer to others on His behalf. Only a loving and intimate relationship with closest familiarity will result in the "good things" that lie latent becoming blatant, influencing others God-wards.

Faith without works is dead is the theme of the letter of James. Perhaps a good paraphrase would be, faith that is only concerned with irrelevancies is not true faith in Christ.

Certainly the believer in Christ should be good, for "this is the will of God for you, even your sanctification." But we also must do good. After all, our Savior was known as a man who "went about doing good," while some of us just go about! We don't even have to go about to do good, there are countless opportunities of doing good right where we are, so long as we separate the important from the irrelevant.

Should we sit in rows or in a semi-circle at the prayer meeting? Should the offering be taken up with a plate or velvet bag? Should we stand up when the minister enters the pulpit? Should we always say the Lord's Prayer or should we sometimes sing it? Should the auditorium lights be dimmed or turned off during the sermon? Should, should, should . . .? All are subjects that have been debated on church premises, sometimes with a great deal of heat engendered. Yet so much time has been expended

GOD'S ANSWER FOR PRESSURE

on these irrelevancies that there has been little or no time to discuss ways and means of evangelism, the true work of the church.

These were Satan's tactics when our Lord was tempted by him. It was Satan's irrelevancies that confronted Christ. It was irrelevant whether he could turn stones into bread—He was the Bread of Life. It was irrelevant whether He could jump from the pinnacle fo the temple and survive—He was the Eternal One. It was irrelevant whether He wanted Satan to give Him all the kingdoms of this world—He owned the world and all that was in it.

Treat irrelevancies as belonging to Satan and don't succumb to their pressure. As one who is in Christ it is the big things that matter.

"Goodness I have none to plead; Sinfulness in all I see, I can only bring my need: God be merciful to me!" Prevent me, O Lord, from becoming bogged down by the small, irrelevant matters. Give me strength to do Your good works that will glorify Your name.

Chapter Twenty-Two

THE PRESSURE OF MATERIALISM

> Blessed . . . with all spiritual blessings in heavenly places in Christ.
>
> Ephesians 1:3

We are living in days when the pressure of materialism is personified by our "Flexible Friends." Special wallets in see-through plastic have been manufactured to hold the more and more credit cards we accumulate. "Charge it!" is the password for convenient car rental, hotel accommodation, restaurant meals, and anything else that once only money could buy. The television commercials are all designed to indoctrinate us into thinking that we cannot, dare not, leave home without our "Flexible Friends."

The day of reckoning, however, comes at the end of the month or quarter when the bank wishes to know how we are going to clear our overdraft!

GOD'S ANSWER FOR PRESSURE

Some modern evangelism does not help the Christian who is under pressure from materialism. It is the healthy, wealthy, and wise Gospel that proclaims, taking text out of context, that "Whatever we ask God for He will give us!" If we want a Rolls Royce then all we do is give God our worn out bicycle (it might just come in useful for some evangelist or missionary!), and ask Him for the Roller—if it doesn't come, and gift-wrapped at that, then it is not God who is at fault but our poor-quality faith.

Our forefathers in the faith used to concentrate, quite rightly, as Paul does in Ephesians, on *spiritual* blessings. Those who are in Christ are "blessed . . . with all spiritual blessings in heavenly places in Christ." Their favorite sermon illustration was: A tramp went up to a man and asked him to "Spare a dime." At that moment he recognized his own father whom he had not seen for many years. The father threw his arms around his son and said, "I've found you; all that I have is yours." There he was, asking for a small coin and he could have a comfortable bed, clean clothes, good food to eat, anything else he desired! Surely an illustration of material mercies? No, our forefathers used to use it as an illustration of spiritual blessings. They hammered the message home with such texts as the one at the top of this chapter. As Christians we need not succumb to the pressure of materialism, for spiritual blessings far outweigh material ones,

THE PRESSURE OF MATERIALISM

for they are "the riches in glory by Christ Jesus."

If we are in Christ, have we entered the "heavenly places" to receive our rightful spiritual blessings? This is not an "out-there" theology. God *is* "out there" but He also is right beside us in the here and now. He is in the "heavenlies" surrounded by superabundant blessings that He is waiting to bestow on us, but He also is right beside us, applying those spiritual blessings to our every condition.

Of course we receive daily material mercies from Him. As a boy I was taught the grace before meat:

For our health and strength and daily food:
We praise Your name, O Lord, Amen.

Food, clothing, shelter, loved ones—all the blessings of this life come from God. In fact, "every good and every perfect gift comes down from above, the Father of lights" (James 1:17). But these are for all. The sun shines through the prison bars upon the wicked, as well as upon the righteous. But spiritual, heavenly blessings are only for those in Christ.

Like our material mercies our spiritual blessings are varied. As we enjoy the beauty of the earth, the wonder of a sunset, the birds, flowers and trees, so as believers in Christ we enjoy pardon and peace, life abundant and answered prayer, the joy of Christian fellowship, and much more. There is no stint with God, either materially or spiritually. He withholds nothing from us that works for our good,

GOD'S ANSWER FOR PRESSURE

only those things that would harm us, and it is only material things that harm, never spiritual blessings.

Because they are spiritual blessings they neither taint nor tarnish. They do not rust or corrode and we cannot be robbed of them. That is one of the pressures of materialism. Our fine belongings and possessions can develop faults, can become damaged, can age. Once we could get them repaired, but now we live in a throw-away age and we have to replace them with something newer and better.

But since our real treasure is spiritual, will it help us to live on earth? Is not our real treasure in heaven waiting for us? Yes and no. Yes, our real treasure is spiritual and there is "an inheritance waiting in heaven, reserved for us, one that never fades." But our spiritual blessings that we are privileged to enjoy here and now, on this earth, help us in a great many ways. They help us to become more spiritual so that one day we shall not feel strange in heaven. They will have prepared us for living in God's "many mansions" or "abiding places" which even now our Lord and Savior is preparing for us.

Don't you wonder, sometimes, why Paul was not more explicit and wrote in more detail about the spiritual blessings in heaven? If he had done so, we might not have understood him! We enjoy the benefits of electricity—light, heat, power—but not many of us understand a generating station or a nuclear powered reactor that produces the electricity. So we may not understand why some

THE PRESSURE OF MATERIALISM

blessings are ours now and some are kept back until eternity, but we can enjoy the ones we have now and enjoy the fact that many more are awaiting us.

Because Christ is "in glory" and "in you," He can give you "all the fullness of the Godhead." Because He considers it best to keep some "on deposit" and let us live out of our "current account" that merely means that He knows best as the Divine Banker.

Our concern should be to "possess our possessions." Instead of wasting time and effort longing for some mysterious blessing we think we should receive in this life, we must possess and enjoy the ones we are receiving daily from His bountiful, generous hands.

Have you never thought that perhaps there were far too many spiritual blessings for Paul to catalog? Or perhaps some of them were too rich and rare for him to describe in prosaic words. Perhaps he did not want to lessen our enjoyment and excitement when we found out what these blessings were for ourselves. That is the pressure of materialism—finding out about more and more things we want, acquiring them, working hard for them, borrowing to buy them, and find we are never satisfied.

But more and more spiritual blessings do no such thing. We can never have a surfeit of them. They do not make us envious, jealous, greedy, prone to trample on others in our search for more and more. All they do is to make us "lost in wonder, love, and praise."

GOD'S ANSWER FOR PRESSURE

Foster your fellowship with Christ. Don't let materialism and the pressures of a worldly spirit spoil your relationship and moment by moment walk with Him. Be content, saying with the hymn writer:

> *How vast the treasure we possess!*
> *How rich Thy bounty, King of grace!*
> Isaac Watts

Thank You, Father, for Your material gifts. They have not failed us day by day. Most of all we thank You for spiritual blessings. Help us to appropriate them more and more, looking ever to that day when we shall receive our inheritance in glory.

Chapter Twenty-Three

THE PRESSURE OF MORTALITY

The dead in Christ shall rise first.
1 Thessalonians 4:16

"I came back from the dead!"

"I died on the operating table and watched them sewing me back together again; then my soul re-entered my body and I was alive again."

"I shall never be afraid of death again after I died in the dentist's chair and came back to life."

These and similar experiences make spectacular reading in the kind of mass market paperbacks that are so popular today, even in Christian circles. I can, however, vouch for the last of the three claims above. He was a teenage boy, the son of my doctor who was a Christian married to another Christian doctor—a real husband and wife team.

This boy died under the anesthetic during a tooth extraction. They sent for his father, who arrived within minutes as his office was only a few doors away from the dentist's. The boy was successfully revived, and his mother and father decided not to tell him that he had "died" and was resuscitated. But several years later, when the son was a university undergraduate, he was talking about mortality to his father and suddenly said, "Dad, do you remember some years ago when I had a tooth out? Well, I died under the anesthetic and my soul ascended to the ceiling and I watched you come into the room and bring me back to life again. I shall never be afraid of death any more for it was quite a wonderful feeling to die."

My own son, after an unknown virus attacked his brain and he became unconscious for nine days, told me when he recovered that he had "died" and that it was a wonderful feeling. He too did not fear death again.

What to make of these out-of-the-body experiences nobody seems to know. Whether they are actual clinical "brain deaths" nobody seems to know. What we do know is that Christ raised people from the dead and He Himself became alive again after the crucifixion.

Another thing that is certain is that all who have found and accepted Christ, who live in Christ, will one day live again in Him.

That life only comes through death is a fact of this natural world in which we live. Our Lord used the analogy when He said, "Unless a corn of wheat fall

THE PRESSURE OF MORTALITY

into the ground and die, it abides alone [remains what it is]: but if it die, it brings forth much fruit." This was true of us spiritually when we became Christians. By receiving Christ we died to our old sinful way of living. It was a spiritual death that resulted in new spiritual life. One day we shall die physically (unless Jesus returns first) and then the result will be entry into a larger, eternal life.

The pressure of mortality is always with us. Every time we switch on the radio or television we hear and see stories about death: death on the roads, death in the sky, death on the sea, death through man's inhumanity to man, and death through disease and old age.

Most people are afraid of man's last enemy, death. As I wrote in my previous book *God's Answer for Fear* (Bridge Publishing, Inc., 1985): "Many of the old Freudian psychoanalysts discovered from the free-association and interpretation of dreams of their patents that they were emotionally disturbed because of a fear of death in their unconscious minds." So what do we do about it? We dress death up in new clothes. We cannot abolish the pressure of mortality, so we try and live with it by calling it different names. In hushed tones we speak of somebody having "passed over," or "he's gone" (without exactly saying where he's gone). We talk of someone having "departed" or "gone to the other side" (the other side of what?). These phrases take away the stark reality of death

GOD'S ANSWER FOR PRESSURE

and relieve the pressure of the spectre of death with his sickle stalking us from behind.

"Death closes all," wrote the poet Tennyson. But for the Christian, death is not a closing door but a door wide open. Beyond the door is the beginning of everything: an eternity with Christ and loved ones who have lived here in Christ. When Jesus returns, writes Paul, those whose bodies are in the grave (and this, of course, includes ashes in an urn for those who have been cremated) will have the privilege of being resurrected first. That number also includes those who have died tragically at sea, in air crashes, in bomb disasters, or in some other equally horrific manner. Having lived in Christ and died in Christ, they will be first to be raised by the returning Lord, to meet Him in the air, their souls (which are even now "with Him, which is far better") being joined to the new resurrection or glorified bodies which the Lord will give them.

Yes, "dead in Christ" implies that first of all we have *lived* in Christ. If living in Him is "life abundant," then what must dying in Him be like? Paul says that "to die is gain" and to be with Christ is "far better." To die in Christ is an experience far excelling living in Him. This then is the scriptural truth that relieves the pressure of our mortality.

I have sat at many Christian deathbeds in my pastoral ministry. Many of them have been thrilling experiences. One in particular stands out in my memory. Sid had been in the hospital for an

THE PRESSURE OF MORTALITY

operation, but the cancer was too extensive. The doctors sewed him up and sent him home to die.

Sid loved his home. Every piece of furniture had been lovingly chosen with his wife. They had enjoyed many years together in that lovely home, and in it they had entertained a host of the Lord's people.

Just before he died he sat upright in bed and spoke for the first time for several days. Smiling at me he said, "I'm going home"—he looked round the home he loved and lay back and died. Home, heaven, the Celestial City, meant much more to him than the house in which he had been living for nearly eighty years.

If we live in Christ then death cannot break our wonderful relationship with our Savior. We shall be much more in Christ when we are with Him. No wonder Paul adds: "Comfort one another with these words." We still sorrow over the parting, but we do not sorrow as "those without hope." We know that a cemetery is the emptiest place on earth for there is nobody there! That was what my father taught me whenever we sat on the top deck of a bus and passed a cemetery. The grave has been a gateway to the "land of pure delight where saints immortal reign!"

Have you ever watched a ship disappear beyond the horizon? "There she goes!" say the onlookers. But remember, on another shore, in another country, there are those waiting to say, "Here she comes!" We may be sad to see a loved one depart to be with the Lord, but other loved ones who have gone before are waiting to welcome them to the worshiping throng around the throne in heaven. Hallelujah!

Teach me, O Lord, to live well and to die well. Prepare me for the great change so that I shall be a fitting partaker of Christ's resurrection, rising to meet Him in the air.

Chapter Twenty-Four

THE PRESSURE OF PROGRESS

The high calling of God in Christ Jesus.
Philippians 3:14

When the first disciples found Christ it was because He called them to Him, to follow Him, to "fish" for Him. Think of your own finding Christ: you came to Him because He was calling you. He may call you through Christian parents, a godly Sunday School teacher, a faithful pastor or zealous evangelist, or even through Christian literature. He calls in many and various ways. But it is always a "high calling," that is, a call to go higher and higher up spiritual paths.

Paul knew that the Philippian Christians were content with the lower, easier paths. They had become slack in their spiritual lives; they were like rowers resting on their oars.

Now we live today in a highly competitive world.

GOD'S ANSWER FOR PRESSURE

Children and students are encouraged and pressured to make good progress, obtaining higher grades, and passing further exams. The young businessman is urged to climb the executive ladder and so "better" himself. For many the ladder of success becomes an awful form of pressure.

On the other hand the Christian is encouraged in the New Testament to grow and progress, not in a competitive sense, but in a Christlike sense, for He "grew in wisdom [mind] and stature [body] and in favor with God [spirit] and man [interpersonal relationships]." It is only as we progress after His pattern and example that we can face up to the pressure to progress in other realms of life.

Having found Christ, then, He calls us to "come up higher," to attainments in the spiritual life that He expects of all who are truly "in Christ." For the Christian "the sky's the limit" for it is a heavenwards calling. In the words of Oswald Chambers it is "my utmost for His highest." Our Savior is,

Christ of the Upward Way,
My guide divine,

Where Thou hast set Thy feet
May I place mine:

And move and march wherever Thou hast trod,
Keeping face forward up the hill of God.

                              W.J. Mathams

THE PRESSURE OF PROGRESS

This high calling is *from* above and *to* above and demands our highest effort. It may be a call to a deeper prayer life. It may be a call to more sacrificial service. It will be a call to closer communion with Christ, for only by becoming more Christlike in character, in personality, in thinking will we have the God-given answer to the pressures of attainment in other realms of life. No wonder Paul describes it as "putting on the Lord Jesus Christ," that is, being clothed with Him so that others see only Him and not us.

Two men had been the closest of friends at school and university. Afterwards they did not meet for many years. When their paths crossed again they found they were quickly bored with each other! They had grown apart; their interests had become different; their circle of friends had changed. So it is possible for the believer and his Lord to grow apart. We allow wrong interests, amusements, pleasures, and people to come between us and our Lord. Friendship with Jesus is subject to the same rules as human friendship. If we neglect Him we become cold and distant or formal in our approach.

Brother Lawrence in his book, *Practicing the Presence of God* tells how he, a monastery cook in a bustling kitchen, learned to make every small chore one of communion with God. So can we. Cleaning the car, digging the garden, shopping in the supermarket, whatever we are doing and wherever we go we can practice the presence. These things no

GOD'S ANSWER FOR PRESSURE

longer become chores but a high calling. No longer do we feel the pressure of keeping up with the Joneses, what we do we "do as to the Lord," not seeking praise for ourselves but rather His glory.

The vocation of the person in Christ is to make daily spiritual progress, becoming so Christlike that the world becomes a better place as we pass through it. The secret is a deeper understanding of the cross.

We entered the Chrisian life through the cross and we progress in that same life by a daily experience of crucifixion—"I die daily" in the words of Paul.

Dorothy was a divorced young mother. Before her divorce she had been subjected to cruel beatings, even though her husband could see how swollen and twisted her arthritic limbs were. She screamed with the pain and walked the streets after each beating. On these walks she often passed our house. She noticed on the front wall by our front door a large-sized crest of Spurgeon's College, London. The design is of a hand holding the cross. The motto beneath read, "I both hold and am held." I made the crest from some left over concrete after constructing a garden path.

After battering Dorothy, her husband would go out on a drinking spree, so soon she was knocking at the door of the house with a cross crest, and we counselled her and advised her for several months.

THE PRESSURE OF PROGRESS

My wife and I believe Dorothy became a woman in Christ.

We then left that church and moved to another in a different part of the country and did not see or hear from Dorothy for over eight years. We often thought of her and prayed for her, remembering the pressures she and her husband were under. The husband kept a small shop in a tiny village. The village had been included with several others into a brand new town, attracting much new commerce and industry. They were now under the pressure to progress syndrome. Somehow they had to restyle the shop and yet keep prices within those of the new town supermarket range. It was then that the divorce occurred, leaving Dorothy with the pressure of progress, the task common to one-parent families, that of bringing up several children through the various stages of growth and education.

Then a wonderful thing happend. The church had never called another minister and so our old Manse or parsonage had been lying vacant. The church decided to rent it and Dorothy applied for it. It was right opposite the church and Dorothy began attending the services and sending the children to Sunday School.

One day she was hanging out the washing on the patio which I had laid when I lived there. Again I had some concrete left over and had been one paving stone short. I filled in the gap with another plaque depicting the college crest. By the time Dorothy

GOD'S ANSWER FOR PRESSURE

moved in the patio was covered with leaves, moss and weeds. However, she swept it and discovered the cross. Tracing my new address and telephone number she rang me to tell me about it. She said that whenever she hung out the washing the message of the cross (holding on and being held) counteracted the pressures of bringing up her children alone. Every visitor to the house was taken down the garden to see the cross! Pressures were lightened as she began a daily dying to self at the cross and then experiencing the power of the living Christ within her.

Think of a mountain goat with its ability to leap and skip over rocks while making progress higher and higher up the mountainside. In a spiritual sense we need this ability, keeping our eyes on the ultimate peak to be reached—intimate fellowship and communion with the God and Father of our Lord Jesus Christ. We are called to Christ to commune with Christ and then we discover like Paul that our fellowship is with the Father and the Son.

O God, I am painfully aware of my lack of spiritual progress. So often I am content with the lower, easier paths. In Your love give me grace to rise and follow You from the lowlands where I have lingered too long to the uplands where I can enjoy all that You have in store for me. Begin a new work of Your Holy Spirit in my life that I may have a greater desire to follow my calling in Christ Jesus.

Chapter Twenty-Five

THE PRESSURE OF RESTITUTION

> Our liberty which we have in Christ Jesus.
>
> Galatians 2:4

Most people find parts of the Bible "heavy going," but many also have trouble with the daily newspaper! Those who can understand the football or racing forecasts or results do not always understand the stocks and shares of the financial pages. So some Christians find Galatians (or "little Romans" as it is sometimes called) one of the "heavier" parts like the book of the Revelation.

The letter to the Galatians is worth persisting with in your devotional studies of God's Word, for it contains a most blessed truth. It describes how, when we have found and accepted Christ as Savior and Lord, we have been set at liberty.

Liberty in the Lord—"If the Son shall make you

free then you shall indeed be free." By living in Christ we are set free from sin and its dominating power; we are freed from all that bound us before we accepted Christ. We are set at liberty from the binding fear of death, failure or the future.

Paul wrote his letter to the Galatians so they might be freed from bondage to Old Testament rites and regulations, laws and libations, ordinances and obligations. In their place he wanted them to know the freedom of the Spirit.

The gospel brings freedom; our acceptance of Christ brings us *into* freedom. What a pity it is when you and I become entangled again "in the yoke of bondage." This is what happens when we come under the pressure and influence of a false cult or we adopt the attitudes of the world around us.

Liberty does not mean license. Living in Christ does not mean we can live as we please and adopt the loose moral standards of the world. No! We live to please Him. We are no longer under the old law, true, but we are under a new law—the law of love. Love for Christ enables us to go further in obedience than love for the law. And love for Christ also results in love for others, so we live for the benefit and blessing of others. This law of love is a great preventative against living selfishly. It helps us to live selfless lives.

One of the pressures we live under is the pressure of revenge. We are tempted to "hit back" and "get even" from a young age. "You wait and see if I

THE PRESSURE OF RESTITUTION

don't . . ." is our taunting reply to someone who has wronged us. Quite often the influence of television is strong at this point. Rarely does a cops-and-robbers end without the robber being taken away in a police car and the criminal shouting out of the window to the officer who arrested him: "You wait, I'll get even with you, I've got friends on the outside."

In chapter ten I told you the story of Daren, the boy who was insecure unless he could collect his "treasures." Let me now tell you about his brother Damen.

Damen was older by several years. He had a wicked temper which appeared uncontrollable at times. There were bouts of kicking and screaming on the floor and neither parent could do much to correct such a tantrum. His one aim in life was to hit back and get even. He would deliberately break his brother's and sister's toys. He would share nothing. If his brother Daren built a tree house then he, Damen, had to have a tree house. If a board fell off his tree house, without waiting to find out if it was a high wind or not, he would tear a plank off his brother's tree house.

Soon he began to get into trouble at school. He was known as a liar and a thief, and on one occasion the police were called in by the headmaster. The parents asked me to try to help although by now Damen had stopped coming to the church services and youth meetings.

I bought some snacks and soda, and took him out

GOD'S ANSWER FOR PRESSURE

for a picnic. Having fed him I talked to him "like a Dutch uncle" (something his father had never done—he had only sworn at him). Finally I set before him the claims of Christ and showed him how different life could be for him if only he would receive Christ as his Savior. With his head he could see the truth of salvation, but his heart would not accept it. He was one of those who thrives on being evil, unkind, and underhanded. "Vengeance is mine, says the Lord" was not for him when he could work out his own schemes of retribution.

Daren has gone into one branch of the armed services and Damen into another. It is to be hoped that the discipline, the *esprit de corps*, and chaplains who preach the gospel, will be able to do something where I failed. How Damen needed to experience that "liberty in Christ," a liberty that is free for us but cost our Savior His life.

Thus we should hold this liberty dearly; it is "God's gift to his own slaves." As we have noted before, as bondslaves of Christ we are servants yet free.

God is love, light, life, *and* liberty. Since He lives in us through His Son, then by being united to Christ we can be loving to others, helping to lighten their path through life. He can take away the urge to hit back and get even, and instead of the pressure of retribution give us the ability to "turn the other cheek."

Look back over your life. How many times have

THE PRESSURE OF RESTITUTION

you thought of paying somebody back for the wrong they did you? Some people I have counseled have been eaten away in their innermost beings by such desires, watching for the right moment, planning what they think is the right act and timing. In many cases they need much inner healing, with Christ being brought into the situation and prayer being offered for release from such damaging emotions.

How Satan loves to hem us in by such pressure. Pride and prejudice, narrow opinions, and a low self-image of ourselves, all contribute to pressure getting the upper hand. The love of hurting others, getting even with them, showing them up, and so on, forges a chain that keeps us in solitary confinement. Who wants to befriend someone so self-centered and vindictive? It is only when Christ is let into our lives that He will let out these oppressing emotions.

Trust Christ to do this. When a person treats you badly and you know you do not deserve such treatment, remember the advice my father used to give me as a boy: "Mud always brushes off when it is dry." Let it take its time drying, they brush it off instead of giving the offending person the "brush-off." As time goes by you will discover how by living in Christ you can let Christ, who is living "in you," take over more and more of the compartments in your life.

At first the freedom He gives may only be accepted on an intellectual level, because you have

GOD'S ANSWER FOR PRESSURE

been told about it, read about it, or heard it preached. Soon it will be a reality deep down within you, affecting every aspect of your life. You will decrease and He will increase—the result: perfect freedom.

Loving, liberating God, Who delivered Your people of old from bondage in Egypt, deliver me from the power of Satan. Help me to do to others what I would like them to do to me. Take away all my desire to hit back and get even. So may I help others to turn to You from the enslaving power of sin.

Chapter Twenty-Six

THE PRESSURE OF SELF-EFFORT

So many of us as were baptized into
Jesus Christ were baptized into his death.
Romans 6:3

"D.I.Y." has become big business. Every city has its Do-It-Yourself (D.I.Y.) center and most supermarkets cater to the enthusiast with a D.I.Y. department or corner. People are eager to paint their own houses, add on a room, or on a humbler scale refinish a table or stool, or build a set of shelves.

There is a great deal of satisfaction in standing back and saying to oneself, "I made that," or even better, showing our handiwork to others.

Of course, there always has been a kind of spiritual D.I.Y. in the realm of morals and religion. Man always has thought that he could be the "Captain of his own salvation." For this reason

GOD'S ANSWER FOR PRESSURE

Scripture emphasizes that salvation is "not of works lest any man should boast." If we could save ourselves by self-effort then God need not have allowed His only Son to die on the Cross of Calvary.

Self-effort is a severe pressure for many people. To be able to claim that we are "a self-made man" is something rather special. That is, until someone deflates us by saying, "Well that relieves the Almighty of a great deal of responsibility!"

It gives us a nice feeling to think that we can reach the top of the ladder of success through our own efforts. In the climb, however, we are subjected to a lot of competition and pressure. Every position at the top in secular work, a job or profession, is competitive and the strain of gaining fresh heights year after year is too much for many people.

In the religious realm it often is the same. There is ecclesiastical one-up-manship (often accompanied by a great deal of "professional" jealousy) among ministers and clergy, elders and deacons, Sunday School teachers, youth leaders, and so on. These things ought not to be. So what is the answer to the pressure of self-effort? Understanding of the believer's position in Christ.

An important part of finding Christ is the realization that finding Him is like putting on a new set of clothes. Compare the text at the heading of this chapter (Romans 6:3) with Galatians 3:27: "For as many of you as have been baptized into Christ have *put on* Christ." It surely reminds us of Isaiah 61:10,

THE PRESSURE OF SELF-EFFORT

"He has clothed me with the garments of salvation." We do not dress ourselves up spiritually, for it is a Divine work.

New clothes often feel strange and restrictive at first. As we wear them, and become accustomed to them, the new clothes feel more and more comfortable. So it is the longer we are in Christ, for the process of becoming in Christ is like a baptism, but not in water, a baptism with the Spirit. This initial Spirit-baptism is a baptism into the Body of Christ. Subsequently there will be many "fillings," equipping us for service and witness and for a display of the fruit of the Spirit and a ministry of the gifts of the Spirit.

This is the very heart of the phrase in Christ. It is nothing less than complete immersion, incorporation, involvement. It is more than believing correct doctrine (important as that is); it is more than being born into a Christian family (wonderful privilege as that is); it is being clothed with Christ by the Holy Spirit, covered from head to foot with His righteousness.

Completely clothed with Christ! That means that God does not look upon us and see us as we see ourselves, full of faults and failings, but He sees us *through* His Son and His righteousness. Does this seem mystical and even mysterious? Then we need to remember that this was Paul writing to the Romans, a very hard-headed and practical people. So this is a very down to earth doctrine for us in this materialistic world in which we live, a world of self-made men and women, business tycoons, up-and-coming executives, and so on. Being in Christ we have been baptized into His death. We must now reckon ourself dead, dead to our old sinful way of life and living "in newness of life." Before reading another word take time to contemplate your own spiritual death and burial. "I live, yet not I," said the apostle Paul. Take no pride in your self-effort, rather thank God for clothing you with Christ.

Frank was a theological student in the late '40s, just after the end of World War II. He was a great admirer of Charles Haddon Spurgeon, the Victorian Baptist preacher. He dressed as closely as he could after the fashion of Spurgeon. Even his black toe-capless shoes (then out of fashion) were replicas of Spurgeon's, as was his black, somber, Sunday-go-to-meeting suit. He grew his hair so that it looked like Spurgeon's, and wore a "broad-brim" hat like the Prince of Preachers. But this was all self-effort. None of it made him even a miniature Spurgeon, except in looks. He could not preach like Spurgeon. The Spirit of God did not use him as Spurgeon was used. And it was not many years before Frank faded out of the full-time ministry altogether, having changed from Spurgeon's denomination to another one!

At the same time, and in the same college was Mark. He was a born mimic. He could mimic all the then well-known London preachers, like

THE PRESSURE OF SELF-EFFORT

Dr. Sangster, for example. He suited his voice to the congregation he was addressing as he went round preaching in different churches. Like Frank, it was all self-effort. He was being pressured into fitting himself into various molds instead of realizing that he was meant to be himself and let the Holy Spirit use what God had made. Mark, too, did not amount to much in the ministry, in the sense that he did not himself become a renowned preacher similar to the ones he was mimicking.

If we are to make Christ real to others we must first be real to ourselves, not endeavoring to make ourselves into somebody or something we are not. The pressure of doing so will be disastrous. The very fact of trying to be something other than God has made us will make us restless, irritated, frustrated, and depressed.

So we do not try to imagine what we can make of ourselves, or do by ourselves. We realize that we are in Christ and wait for the Holy Spirit who baptized us into Christ to make of us what He wants and to do with us what He wishes. No way can we make ourselves into preachers of renown, or successful evangelists, or fervent prayer warriors, or enthusiastic missionaries. Such people are those who are in Christ, baptized into Him, the self crucified, and relying upon the Spirit-baptizer to do His own work within us.

Many people get into trouble with their D.I.Y. schemes. Sometimes it is with gas, electricity, or water and the experts have to be called in to make good the damage. What began as a money-saving scheme ends by becoming rather costly. The cost will be equally great if we persist in using self effort in the Christian life. In the words of the old Keswick Convention slogan it is "Let go and let God."

Loving God, I thank You for my Savior who died for my sins and was buried but rose again from the dead. I thank You that through the baptism of the Spirit I have been united to Christ and His Church. Thank You, too, for my water baptism, the outward sign of receiving this inward grace. Please give me all joy and peace in beieving, and a continual infilling of Your Holy Spirit.

Chapter Twenty-Seven

THE PRESSURE OF TIMIDITY

That I might be much bold in Christ.
Philemon 1:8

Living in Christ should affect our whole being, body, mind, and spirit, our physical, intellectual, spiritual, and emotional life. Boldness is a somewhat rare emotion among Christians, the counterpart of timidity or cowardice. Even the young Timothy suffered from it. Paul wrote to encourage him and told him not to "blush, then, for the witness thou bearest to our Lord" (2 Timothy 1:8). It took a Catholic translator, Ronald Knox, to come up with such a striking and convicting translation! Do we blush when witnessing? Do we live beneath the pressure of timidity, natural or acquired?

Paul was affected by this pressure too. Frequently he asked his fellow Christians to pray that he might be bold in his proclamation of the gospel.

GOD'S ANSWER FOR PRESSURE

Physical danger in the world is one thing; that often can be counteracted by physical courage. But moral courage is quite another thing. A soldier in the heat of battle often can equip himself well, and perform a brave deed in the face of overwhelming odds. But to stand up and be counted as a Christian in a non-Christian society is another matter.

The early Christian martyrs, from Stephen onwards, knew the pressure of timidity. They did not go to the lions with relish and strong limbs. It was the lions who licked their lips with relish and sprang forward on strong legs. So too the fire licking the stake began to burn the bodies of men and women who naturally were timorous, but supernaturally were given "boldness in Christ" for their ordeal and witness to Christ. So today there are those in communist dominated countries who are naturally timorous, but who suffer imprisonment and brainwashing techniques with supernatural fortitude, to the astonishment of their captors.

Most of us will not have to face lions, the stake, a firing squad, or a solitary cell. But how do we fare when faced with cheating on exams in college or university? Do we possess moral bravery in the face of drugs, pornography, or the Satanic "fiery darts" of doubt and perplexity when confronted by agnostics, atheists, or humanists?

The apostle Paul's pressure of timidity took the form of writing a much needed letter to the owner of a runaway slave. On a half-sheet of paper,

THE PRESSURE OF TIMIDITY

approximately 300 words, he set out fifteen reasons why Philemon should take back his runaway slave Onesimus. The letter is a masterpiece of Christian courtesy, dignity, and restraint, at the same time being a lesson to us today in how to overcome timidity. In Christ he knew he need not succumb to the pressure of timidity. He could write to Philemon with a holy boldness, pleading for forgiveness and restoration on behalf of Onesimus.

Perhaps you need to write a letter, interrupting the reading of this book to do so. Maybe you are too cowardly to put pen to paper. Is the pressure of timidity too strong as you think of the friend you have wronged? Or perhaps God has been showing you that some younger man or woman in your church could do your piece of Christian service more effectively. How hard it is to discover that God wants someone else in our place and a letter of resignation would be the right thing to do. The pressure of thinking we are indispensable is as great as the pressure of being too cowardly to take a back seat gracefully!

What of that son or daughter who has left home and you failed to warn them of their indifference to spiritual things. Are you too timid to write that long overdue letter setting out your own personal convictions about Christ and how they might come to love Him and serve Him? Only life in Christ can provide the incentive and the inspiration to write such a letter. However delicate the subject matter the Holy Spirit (given to us as our Helper as soon as we become in Christ) can give us holy boldness. It will not be the world's boldness, which often is rudeness, calling a spade a spade for its own sake. But rather a sympathetic feeling for the finer feelings of others. Boldness in Christ is never synonymous with worldly rudeness.

Boldness for Paul was always forthrightness tempered with love. When we speak about Christians today needing to speak out with moral bravery against the evils of our time we must be like our Savior who hated sin but loved the sinner. The apostle Paul could have offended Philemon by writing a letter denouncing slavery. Instead he wrote about brotherly love that makes slavery meaningless.

General Booth's wife wrote a book which she entitled *Love is All*. Yes, love is all we need in our fight against evil; love that tempers our boldness with courtesy. Love without boldness gives the wrong image of Christianity, making it out to be sickly and effeminate. Boldness without love also gives the wrong impression, making Christianity out to be hard and ruthless. But boldness with love, the courage and charity of Christ, tempered with His mind and Spirit, makes Christianity attractive. "Speaking the truth in love" should be our biblical motto and aim.

Such boldness comes through seeing the power of love in action. That is how Jesus dealt with the

THE PRESSURE OF TIMIDITY

problems of His day. "Love your neighbour as yourself," He said. Love was His answer for friction between friends, and factions among neighbors. The building of that garage, the heightening of that wall or fence, the pruning of those overhanging branches, these so-called drastic acts by near neighbors can all be resolved by loving boldness. "Love your enemies," said Jesus. Love and boldness not only resolve differences between neighbors and friends, but between nations. "Love one another," said Jesus. Try it. Ask the Holy Spirit to help you overcome your timidity and see if your relationships with people at home, at work, at play, do not improve.

Today's language has birthed the new term, doubletalk. Many people hide what they really want to say beneath a wall of words. What we actually hear them saying is not what they really want to say if they were only true to their inner feelings. It becomes verbal distortion, or doubletalk. Because of the pressure of timidity, caused through shyness, lack of self-worth, fear of criticism, or giving offense, people say things other than they mean, other than they would really like to say.

Trying to be loving, honest, and truthful is extremely difficult in combination. We know that if we are truthful about Mrs. Jones' hat we shall offend her! If we really say what we think about Mr. Jones' do-it-yourself shelving, he probably will never hammer in another nail! So we descend to white lies, forgetting that all lies are black and that the sin of lying is condemned in Scripture. Only by living in Christ, moment-by-moment, will we know just what to say in such embarrassing situations, without hiding behind a wall of words or giving offense because we are too "John Blunt." If we would read the third chapter of the letter of James more frequently we should talk more effectively, "peaceably," "without partiality," and "without hypocrisy," with "boldness in Christ Jesus."

Help me so to speak, O God, that my words will be a blessing to others. Help me to write so that my letters might be messages of love and wisdom. Take away my timidity and give me opportunities to speak boldly yet courteously about my Savior, commending His love to all with whom I come into contact. Bless me that I might become a blessing to many.

Chapter Twenty-Eight

THE PRESSURE OF TOGETHERNESS

You are all one in Christ Jesus.
Galatians 3:28

Do you suffer from ecumania? Don't worry, it's not fatal!

"Ecumania" is a word to describe people who are so absorbed by the idea of a visible, organizational unity of the universal Christian Church that they seem to have little time or thought for anything else. Such people have usually succumbed to pressure of togetherness from those "at the top"— denominational headquarters, local or national councils of churches, and the like. There seems little interest for such unity at the grassroots, among the ordinary church members of the various denominations, but a great deal of advice and opinion is given from above. Thus many churches and church councils are pressured about togetherness.

GOD'S ANSWER FOR PRESSURE

Those at the top often forget that we like to have different wallpaper from our neighbors, and we like to drive different cars. It would be a very drab world if we all had the same interior decoration and drove about in the same make and color of car. We are of differing tastes and personalities, and so we like to live with variety. Our clothes and belongings are chosen according to our taste and to express our personality. And in the same way, some like "high church" worship with plenty of dressing-up, bells and smells and ritual. Others like a non-conformist liturgy that allows for spontaneous prayers, for instance. Yet others prefer a charismatic type of free worship, body worship in both senses of the word: worship in which all members of the Body can take part, and in which the body can express worship through dance, for instance. If all such differing modes of worship were combined within one church fellowship and one church building it would be a strange kind of hybrid indeed.

The onset of ecumania usually is caused by a misunderstanding of our Lord's words, "That they all may be one" (John 17:21). The quotation is, of course, incomplete, and has to be taken in context. Jesus was praying that all Christians might be one *in the same way as He and His Father were one.* In other words they *already were one*; He was praying that the existing unity might become stronger and deeper. So Pauls's statement in Galatians 3:28 is in keeping with the prayer of the Lord, "You *are* all

THE PRESSURE OF TOGETHERNESS

one in Christ." There already exists unity (not uniformity) between believers. This unity is seen at conventions for the deepening of spiritual life, such as the Keswick Convention. The same unity already exists and is manifest when believers of all denominations (and none) support an evangelistic campaign on a city-wide basis, such as when Dr. Billy Graham conducts one.

The pressure of togetherness exerted by those who would mold us after the same pattern and incorporate us into a vast world-church is unnecessary and unscriptural. You already are united, wrote Paul to the Galatians, for as individuals you all are in Christ, so together. When we pray, work, and witness together in acts of evangelism, we all are one in Christ Jesus. Our in-Christ-ness is the cement or mortar that binds us together, not the pressure created by some council or committee.

All those living in Christ possess the same common life, the resurrection life of the Lord Himself. Whatever may be our class, color, or Christian creed; whatever denominational label we may wear (or none); whichever missionary society we support; whatever hymn book we choose to sing from; whichever modern translation of the Bible we read—these make not the slightest difference to our essential unity in Christ:—

> *Names, and sects, and parties fall,*
> *Thou O Christ art All-in-all.*
>   Charles Wesley

GOD'S ANSWER FOR PRESSURE

Everyone who reads this book, whether belonging to one of the traditional denominations or members of a charismatic community church or Restoration Church, has a spiritual kinship with each other. You have never met one another, but you all have met the same risen Lord. You all know the same joy and delight of living in Him. You and I have been "baptized into Christ," whether you think that means water-baptism or Spirit-baptism, and so we share this close, intimate relationship. We enjoy a togetherness with no pressure from without for it comes from within, the same indwelling Holy Spirit who fills all Christians. There is no pressure, for all artificial distinctions are nothing to do with our being all one in Christ Jesus.

Although Paul is talking about a spiritual unity it still is a unity that can be exhibited to the world, without us being pressured into one building, worshiping in one way. The first disciples were called "Christians" first in the city of Antioch. One day the populace of Antioch noticed some men and women who were miniature Christs, passable imitations of Him, and so they called them Christ-ones or Christians. They were not called Baptists even though they had been baptized on profession of their faith by immersion in water. They were not called Methodists, even though their methodical pattern of living commended itself to all. They were not referred to as Adventists even though they sincerely believed in the imminent return of their

THE PRESSURE OF TOGETHERNESS

Lord. Because they met to break bread on the first day of the week, that did not provide a nickname. Because they exercised the gifts of the Spirit and exhibited the graces of the Spirit that did not label them charismatics. They were named Christians because they were so like Jesus Christ. The people of Antioch could see that they lived in Christ.

The bounds of unity cannot be fixed by men. They already are arranged by God. Those living in Christ are all one in Christ. But we can deepen the unity that already exists, perhaps by arranging more events in which we can all take part without detriment to our particular denominational or non-denominational emphases. Our divisions do not matter so long as we confess the essentials and agree on the essentials: Christ's deity and death, Christ's resurrection and return; salvation by grace, through faith. Believing the fundamentals without compromise, there is no need to compromise to get together—we are together. Our honest differences are about secondary issues and need not destroy our unity. As a wise man once said: "The closer Christians get to Christ, the closer they get to one another."

We are walking together along the same road, a route that leads to heaven. While we walk we share what we can; love all we can; evangelize all we can. Walking in unity means absolute honesty, transparent honesty, and all transcendent love. Christians can and must share a love-life, a life of love in Christ, putting Christ first, others second, and ourselves last.

A man expressed it to me recently like this, when asked to which church he belongs. His reply was as follows: "I'm an Anglican because I believe their creed; I'm a Baptist because I believe in baptism by immersion; I'm a Congregationalist because I believe in church independency; I'm a Pentecostal because I believe in the gifts of the Spirit; I'm a Methodist because I believe in a disciplined life; I'm a Presbyterian because I believe in elders; I'm a Quaker because I believe in peace; I'm a Restorationist because I believe Jesus is coming again to restore the kingdom; I'm a Salvationist because I believe in open-air preaching."

I knew that by upbringing and conviction he was a member of the Christian Brethren. They do not believe in a one-man-ministry and also believe in welcoming all the Lord's people to their meetings. His was a truly "all one in Christ Jesus" unity that incorporated all who were in Christ and excluded none. He knew no pressure of human togetherness; his togetherness was Spirit-engendered.

Most gracious God, You who are three Persons united in one, continue to prosper the unity of Your people, that all who are in Christ may truly sing: "We are not divided, All one body we, One in hope and doctrine, One in charity."

Chapter Twenty-Nine

THE PRESSURE OF UNCERTAINTY

> Since we heard of your faith in Christ Jesus.
>
> Colossians 1:4

We cannot remind ourselves too often that we have accepted Christ by faith—"For by grace are you saved, through faith." Now faith is not, as a schoolboy once said, "Believing what you know isn't true!" Nor is it a "leap in the dark." Faith in the Bible is both intellectual assent, and belief in the heart.

Enoch, in the Old Testament, "walked by faith in the most intimate fellowship with his Lord," once said a famous preacher. Enoch never ran ahead nor did he lag behind. Step by step he walked in heavenly communion with God, and one day the path of faith led him to the gateway of glory and "he was not, for God took him." One small child in Sunday School described Enoch's end like this:

GOD'S ANSWER FOR PRESSURE

"God said, 'Enoch, you have walked a long way today, instead of returning home you'd better come home with me!'" What a reward for walking by faith.

Hebrews 11 is the most famous chapter in the New Testament about heroes of faith, and Enoch is one of them. It is a good exercise to read the chapter, then make two columns on a sheet of paper. In the left hand column list the uncertainties of life surrounding these men and women, and then in the right hand column list how their faith expressed itself. For instance, there was Abraham with a barren wife, yet he had faith to believe he would father many descendants. There was Moses, taken away from his parents three months after he was born, but his faith made him leader of God's people, leading them through the Red Sea and the wilderness.

The text in Romans which was instrumental in the conversion of Martin Luther ("The just shall live by faith") implies more than being raised from the deadness of sin to eternal life. It implies also that the Christian life is kept going through living by faith.

A father watched three small children walking "catlike" along the top of a high brick wall. Soon they felt dizzy and afraid of falling. Running to the wall he shouted, "Jump into my arms." Two jumped and one hesitated. The one who hesitated was only a friend. The two who jumped were his own son and daughter. The father's children trusted him

THE PRESSURE OF UNCERTAINTY

immediately. They knew their father's love, strength, and desire to help them.

As we continue to live by faith, so we shall get to know our Savior more and more, and trust Him more and more. As Jesus entrusted Himself to His Father on the cross, so we shall be willing to trust ourselves to Him for daily living. Sometimes we shall feel like the three children, afraid of falling, until we remember that He holds us in the hollow of His hand. Then we shall want to sing:

> *When I fear my faith will fail,*
> *Christ will hold me fast;*
> *When the tempter would prevail,*
> *He can hold me fast.*
>
> *I could never keep my hold,*
> *He must hold me fast;*
> *For my love is often cold,*
> *He must hold me fast.*
>
> R. Harkness

What an uncertain world we live in. Our health is uncertain with one in four developing cancer. Our wealth is uncertain with more and more people without jobs. Life itself is uncertain, living as we do beneath the threat of nuclear holocaust. Dangers on the road, disasters in the air and on the sea. Erupting volcanoes, hurricanes, famines, friends who fail us when we least expect them to do so—all these uncertainties surely drive us to One who is "not a disappointment," Jesus Christ.

GOD'S ANSWER FOR PRESSURE

Faith has been called "the essence of the Christian life in its Godward aspect." Our daily prayer should therefore be: "Lord, increase our faith." How illogical it is to think we can begin the Christian life by faith and then continue without it. If it was our preliminary faith in Christ that saved us, then it is our persistent faith that enables us to continue with a consistent daily walk.

How do we persevere in faith amidst all the uncertainties of life? I have found Bible memory texts to be the best help, and over the years I have devised the following system. Taking the twenty-six letters of the alphabet, I find in a concordance twenty-six Bible texts beginning with each letter. Photo-copying the list I keep one in various places, such as my diary. During the year I have then learned twenty-six different texts of Scripture. Mind you, it is difficult with X and Z ringing the changes over the years! I get round X by selecting such texts as "eXamine yourselves, if you be in the faith; prove yourselves. Know you not how that Jesus Christ is in you" (2 Corinthians 13:5)! These texts I can quote to myself during any time of uncertainty.

Often when I lie awake at night, thinking over the uncertainties that surround us all, I begin at A and silently quote to myself my texts. Long before I have got to Z, I usually am fast asleep!

What a difference our "faith in Christ Jesus" will make not only to us but to our home and family, our village or town, our office or factory, our school or

THE PRESSURE OF UNCERTAINTY

college. One Bible commentator says of Paul's words in Colossians 1:4, "They were in Christ, and they were in Christ in Colossae. Colossae became a different place as they looked at it from the shelter of Christ." Yes, a deep inner spiritual life can transform all that is outward. This is not like the man of the world who sometimes looks at life through "rose-colored spectacles." The outer world appears not merely a better place, it actually does become better. As faith changes the person so, it transforms the world around him, relieving the pressure of uncertainty, replacing it with faith in Christ.

As our faith in Christ begins to mature and grow stronger so will our vision as to what God can do in response to our faith. Today many Christians have no vision, except *television!* If we compare ourselves with such men of vision as George Mueller or Hudson Taylor how far short we fall. The former founded and fed an orphanage on faith alone. The second founded the China Inland Mission (now the Overseas Missionary Fellowship), the missionaries of which all lived by relying on the Lord alone to supply their needs. "What an uncertain existence," some critics said. Yet, for them there was no uncertainty, for their faith was "mountain-moving" faith, for it was "faith in Christ Jesus."

GOD'S ANSWER FOR PRESSURE

Our Father, We thank You that by faith we are saved; by faith we stand; by faith we live. We praise You that in an uncertain world we can be certain of You and Your love. Deepen our faith, broaden our vision, that we might become "men true of heart and strong in faith."

Chapter Thirty

THE PRESSURE OF WORLDLINESS

> The simplicity [sincerity] that is in Christ.
>
> 2 Corinthians 11:3

The poet William Wordsworth knew something of the pressure of worldliness when he wrote: "The world is too much with us; late and soon, Getting and spending, we lay waste our powers."

A customer in a florist's shop heard a bell ring while waiting to be served. The proprietor called out "Frost!" and left the customer waiting in the shop while he ran to the greenhouse. Returning, he explained that an electric device warned when the temperature in the greenhouse dropped to a danger level when frost was about. Many of his flowers were thus saved from an untimely end.

Paul's words in 2 Corinthians 11:3 are like a frost bell for the Christian. Knowing that the world

GOD'S ANSWER FOR PRESSURE

around us can give us spiritual frostbite, leaving us cold and stiff instead of being devoted to Christ with fervent zeal, he writes, "The simplicity [or sincerity] that is in Christ," that is, the man or woman in Christ is living in Him with genuine, warm-heated devotion. As Jesus criticized the Church of Laodicea for its lukewarmness, so He dislikes seeing us with cold hearts and formal religion. He wants us to be on fire for Him, with love and service.

This is the kind of love that will allow no rival to have a place in our hearts. Read the lives of men like Hudson Taylor, George Mueller, and Charles Haddon Spurgeon and you will find that they all told their brides that they would have to take second place to Christ and His Church. But such a place given to Christ is not only for the prominent people. For all who are in Christ He "must have the pre-eminence." Not only must Jesus be prominent in our lives, He must be pre-eminent. He must take precedence over pleasure, position, power, and all other things coveted by non-Christians. None of these things must be allowed to intrude into the throne room of the heart where Jesus only should reign. If Jesus begins to be pushed out, then the cold frost of worldliness will settle and soon turn into a big freeze-up.

Paul lists the freeze-up of the Christian as being due to "the world, the flesh, and the devil." Note his order. How we like to think we are engaged in a fearsome battle with Satan and the unseen powers

THE PRESSURE OF WORLDLINESS

of darkness. Well, we are, as Paul tells us in Ephesians chapter six. But it is so convenient to blame everything on Satan and see his demons everywhere as some continually see "Reds under the beds." It is much harder to acknowledge that many of the things wrecking our spiritual lives are due to the pressure of worldliness. To admit that means that we must do something about it. It is easier to blame the devil than to blame our own selfish worldly inclinations.

As Christians we are *in* the world, but not *of* the world. Being in the world means we take our place in society. Not being of the world means we do not adopt some of the standards and pressures of that same society. The apostle John was in complete agreement with Paul, stating, "Love not the world, neither the things of the world" (1 John 2:15). James concurred with them, stating, "Don't you know that the friendship of the world is enmity with God?" (James 4:4).

So when the world presses down on us, trying to squeeze us into its mold, then we remember that we are loved with fervent sincerity by Christ, and we must love Him with equal intensity, the fervency thus melting the frost and ice of worldly pressures.

We are not therefore called to become isolationists, living like hermits in a cell, remote from life and indifferent to others around us. But it does mean that we shall be like the Gulf Stream in the Atlantic, maintaining a warm temperature in the midst of the icy waters round about. We shall not become "conformed" to the world but "transformed" by the love of Christ. Our lives will act as leaven, salt, and light, effectively changing the world around us.

Noel knew that he should be like leaven, salt, and light, yet working on a farm among Christians he seemed to have no contact with the dark world that needed his light. After praying about it he decided to join a football team and a squash club. That did not mean that he had to go in for the drinking bouts and woman-chasing of others on the team. He still kept his Christian standards and followed Christ closely, consistently, and constantly. The other members of the football club and squash club watched him closely. When they saw his "sincerity that [was] in Christ Jesus" they came to him with their problems. Whereas before he lived in virtual isolation on the farm, with no one to invite to church services, now he was able to invite several with whom he came into contact at the leisure center.

As the world begins to see transformed individuals, they will want the transforming power of Christ in their own lives, and so gradually the world becomes transformed. Worldliness is not a list of doubtful pleasures and amusements such as drinking, drugs, dancing, the theater, the television, and so on. Worldliness is the adoption by the Christian of worldly attitudes, standards, and mentality, seeing everything in terms of serving the self.

THE PRESSURE OF WORLDLINESS

"Sincerity in Christ." This sincerity comes only from Christ. He imparts it to those who are in Him. The word "sincere" means quite literally "without wax." In ancient Roman times a sculptor filled in flaws with wax. A sculpture without wax was said to be "sincere" or *sine* (without), *cerus* (wax). How sincere an image of Christ do we present to the world? Are there flaws in our character or in our conduct? Are there flaws in our thinking? Are there flaws in our manner of speech? If our love for Christ is sincere then it will result in a perfect image of Him, genuine and not counterfeit.

This means that we have to be honest with ourselves. If only Satan was our trouble then we could rely on the prayer and power of the Spirit all the time. But as we have seen worldliness is a different sort of enemy. We have to take a stand, resist, take positive measures ourselves, with, of course, God's help. We have to make an honest assessment as to how and how much the pressure of the world is affecting our Christian life and testimony. In our choice of clothes, the sort of holiday we select, the car we buy, the luxuries we surround ourselves with in our homes—these might all be a copy fo the trends and lifestyles of the people of the world around us. It may make us squirm a little (or even a lot), to be so honest with ourselves, but this introspection is necessary if we are to live according to "the sincerity that is in Christ."

GOD'S ANSWER FOR PRESSURE

O Lord, forgive my worldly tendencies. Free me from the pressure of worldly pleasures, position, and power. Help me to do without, so that I may be of help to some who are lacking the bare necessities of life. As Jesus had no home, nowhere to lay His head, and once had to borrow a Roman coin, make me less dependent on material comforts and possessions.

Chapter Thirty-One

THE PRESSURE OF YESTERYEAR

> There is therefore now no condemnation to them that are in Christ Jesus.
> Romans 8:1

Have you really found Christ, *really* found Him? What a thrilling discovery it is. It is like the man in the New Testament who was a merchant looking for fine pearls. One day he found a pearl of particularly great value and sold everything he possessed in order to buy it. Jesus, according to the hymn-writer James Mason, is the "Pearl of Greatest Price" and the one who finds Him must sing:

I've found the pearl of greatest price!
My heart doth sing for joy;
And sing I must, for Christ is mine!
Christ shall my song employ.

GOD'S ANSWER FOR PRESSURE

I do not mean finding Him as a good man or an example to be copied. I mean finding Him as a Savior; One who can live in you from day-to-day, as you live in Him. "We have found Him," shouted Andrew to his brother and Philip to Nathanael, by the lakeside, and by finding Him they discovered His salvation.

Paul, the expert on Christ-mysticism, on being in Christ, found Him on the road to Damascus. And for Paul salvation was eternal. His letter to the Romans begins (chapter 8) with "no condemnation" and ends with "no separation." Jesus both saves and keeps. He deals with the past, the present, and the future.

The pressures of the past often dominate a person's living in the present and can make life utterly miserable. "I've forgotten myself but I can't forget what I did," is a common complaint. We should rather say, "God has forgiven me and therefore I can forget." We must not let the memory of past sins rob us of joy in the present.

Normal regret sometimes turns into obsession if we do not consciously think through the implications of being in Christ. Having acknowledged our sins, repented of them, and trusted in Christ's death for us on the cross of Calvary, then there is no need to keep their memory alive. We must focus on what Christ has done and not on what we have done. When He forgives we can forget. Guilt is a burden that God does not intend His children to bear.

THE PRESSURE OF YESTERYEAR

Memories of the past can take a toll on the emotions and such pressure can cause untold strain. Remember, you have been acquitted from past sin as if in a court of law. By His death Christ pardoned you; by His resurrection He empowers you to deal with the pressure of temptation in the future. Christ "in you" and "you in Christ" means a *living* Christ has taken up residence within you and you are "alive in Christ." Your sins have been condemned, but not you.

This is good news for the alcoholic, the sexual pervert, the drug addict, and all who are under pressure because of their past way of life. It was good news to Leonard, a man whose wife had left him. He still loved her dearly and whenever he had access to the children he tried for reconciliation. The trouble was his mother-in-law "ganged up" with her daughter against him. He was reminded again and again by her of what she considered his faults and failings were that had caused her daughter to leave him.

Leonard began to develop panic attacks. Depression set in. He tried jumping out of a window and other ways of committing suicide. Drugs from the doctor did not relieve the pressure. Electroconvulsive treatment was tried with no effect. Talking with me he said, "I know nobody understands my feelings, my hurtful emotions, my dreadful fears. Sometimes I wish my head had a little flap in it and that the doctors could lift it and see into my brain and understand all that is happening in my head.

"I know that there is only God left. I've tried medicine, psychiatry, and all the rest, but God has got to deal with my pressures."

It took him many months of spiritual counseling, of healing of memories, of attendance at quiet, worshipful services before he felt God lifting the pressure and giving him peace about the past.

Complete liberation often is not realized at once. Frequently it is a slow process. When we come to Christ for forgiveness from the past we become mere "babies in Christ"; there must follow a daily "growing up into Christ," not remaining stunted, underdeveloped or spiritually immature.

If you have found Him, and have begun to enjoy being in Him, then you will want to go deeper and deeper into a more enriching fellowship. You will not be content to settle for a minimum Christianity. In a micro-chip mini-age you will want the maximum. To be in Christ implies complete involvement, a total absorption of ourselves in Jesus Christ. It is more than being saved from hell and saved for heaven, it is you and me being deeply involved with Christ in the everyday affairs of life so that the pressures do not destroy us.

This is such a thrilling experience that, like Paul, you will have a measure of regret that you did not find Him earlier in life. Paul wrote of those who were "in Christ *before me*," thus making him envious.

THE PRESSURE OF YESTERYEAR

Such were Rob and Elaine. They came to know Christ in middle life. Their transformation was tremendous. Their married life took such a turn for the better that they said to me, "We wish you could marry us all over again." But their great happiness was marred by pressure from the past. As they looked back over the wasted years they felt that their present service for Christ was almost insignificant. It was only after hearing a sermon on Joel 2:25 ("I will make up to you the years that the locusts have eaten") that they were encouraged to forget the past and live victoriously in the present.

So we must first find Him, then invite Him to enter into our innermost being. He has said, "Behold, I stand at the door and knock." So open the door of your life and let Him walk in. He also said, "I am the door," so you walk in.

Finding Christ. Have you found Him? He said, "Seek and you shall find." Remember, He is "a rewarder of those who diligently seek Him."

A wise king wrote, "Those who seek me early shall find me." The earlier the better. Early in life is the best time to discover this life and union with Christ, before the pressures of life have a chance to accumulate and mount up like a pile of rubble.

But if you have not found Christ early in life, never think it is too late. I had just finished preaching and was packing up my things to go home when an elderly lady came to the vestry. She asked me, "Am I too late?" Thinking she did not want to delay my home-going, I said, "I've always got time to talk to people about spiritual things." "No," she said, "am I too old to become a Christian? I am over eighty years of age." There and then she entered into Christ and was later baptized. As the pressures of the past were lifted she entered into a joyful relationship with her Lord. She could not go to enough meetings where her soul would be fed on God's Word. She even attended the Youth Fellowship as well as the Ladies' Meeting and the church prayer meeting and Bible study. The Lord graciously restored her years that the locusts had eaten!

Lord, Jesus, please forgive my godless past. Help me to find You and then to get nearer to You. Help me to love You with all my heart. Let me walk with You in love, work for You with energy, and if need be suffer for You with patience. Lord, live in me, and let me live in You.